WILDERNESS
AXE SKILLS AND CAMPCRAFT

Design and layout Copyright © BlueRed Press Ltd. 2021
Text and photography Copyright © Paul Kirtley 2021

Library of Congress Control Number: 2020943458

Produced by BlueRed Press Ltd. 2020
Interior design by Insight Design Concepts Ltd.
Type set in Berling

ISBN: 978-0-7643-6148-7
Printed in China
5 4 3 2

Published by Schiffer Publishing, Ltd.
4880 Lower Valley Road
Atglen, PA 19310
Phone: (610) 593-1777; Fax: (610) 593-2002
Email: Info@schifferbooks.com
Web: www.schifferbooks.com

For our complete selection of fine books on this and related subjects, please visit our website at www.schifferbooks.com. You may also write for a free catalog.

Schiffer Publishing's titles are available at special discounts for bulk purchases for sales promotions or premiums. Special editions, including personalized covers, corporate imprints, and excerpts, can be created in large quantities for special needs. For more information, contact the publisher.

We are always looking for people to write books on new and related subjects. If you have an idea for a book, please contact us at proposals@schifferbooks.com.

WILDERNESS
AXE SKILLS AND CAMPCRAFT

 Paul Kirtley

SCHIFFER
PUBLISHING

4880 Lower Valley Road • Atglen, PA 19310

Dedicated to my parents, Tom and Gina, who allowed me to play in the woods as a child, and to my partner, Amanda, who encourages me to keep playing in the woods as an adult.

Contents

Introduction

Woodcraft is the first of all the sciences. It was Woodcraft that made man out of brutish material, and Woodcraft in its highest form may save him from decay.
—Ernest Thompson Seton

Being able to fashion items from wood is one of our oldest skills. Wooden items don't survive in the archeological record as commonly as stone, bone, or antler artifacts, but it stands to reason that if we were shaping these harder materials, we were also shaping wood. Flint spearpoints would have needed hafting, and flint arrowheads needed arrow shafts. Digging sticks, spear throwers, and stone axe and adze handles all would naturally have been fashioned from wood.

From archeological evidence, it's understood humans have been able to create and control fire for hundreds of thousands of years. Even the act of selecting and collecting kindling and firewood provides a deeper understanding of the materials. Which species break easily, which of them spring back when bent, which are heavy, which are light, which are full of resin, which burn quickly and brightly, and which burn with a more steady heat, leaving hot embers? Wood has always been in our hearths and continues to be.

Metal changed our relationship with wood. Sharp and durable edges refined and redefined what was possible, and what could be produced in a given time. Both speed of manufacture and quality of finish are generally increased when using metal tools over their older predecessors. Many European cultures have long-established and deep traditions of woodworking. Many of the tools we use, such as the knife, the axe, and the adze, have their origins in stone tools. Just as metal tools increased the quality and extent of woodcraft in the places metal was discovered, the propagation of high-quality steel with exploration, trade, and colonialism changed the landscape of native woodcraft of the indigenous peoples encountered.

This book arose from the syllabus of a course I teach, called The Woodcrafter. The aim of the course is to equip students with a solid foundation of wilderness axe techniques and a range of campcraft knowledge to serve them in varied woodland environments. The subjects

Left: *The author on a lakeside camping spot, applying simple yet effective firewood-splitting techniques.*

included fit together in a coherent way but also augment other courses I teach, in particular the Elementary Wilderness Bushcraft course. Likewise with this book, the aim is to describe a set of knowledge and techniques that sit together in a coherent way, which makes sense to present in one piece. Of course, the decision to include or exclude particular topics in a book is in part a personal choice, but also subject to the constraints of the format.

I should mention this is not a book of basic bushcraft techniques. Fire making, fire management, leaving fire sites safe, and finding water and making it safe, for example, are all skills it's assumed the reader is proficient in. In some ways the reader should think of the majority of the techniques in this book as ones added after the basics, layered on top of the elementary bushcraft skills.

Bushcraft, woodcraft, camping, and wilderness-living skills can be sliced and diced in so many ways that in any book there will undoubtedly be topics or techniques that can't be included. My hope is that there is information in this book that is new to you, shows a higher level of skill or refinement or efficiency than you've seen before, presents more-familiar subjects in a fresh way, or fills in needed details that are hard to find elsewhere.

In considering the subjects covered in this book, I haven't included techniques I don't use. This is not necessarily because they are bad or inferior, only that any book can't contain every way you might invent for doing something. Equally it would be disingenuous of me to teach something in an authoritative fashion when I have little experience with it. At the time of writing, we live in a day and age when there is so much shared information on the internet, some of it great and inventive and some of it useless, dangerous, or lacking context. Yet, there is an existing body of knowledge that is verified and validated. There is a tradition of using particular techniques in a particular way with particular resources, because that's what works in a real context. In some cases this knowledge has been hard won in the face of the laws of nature. In all cases the techniques are repeatable and have stood the test of time.

I didn't invent the skills I'm sharing here. Yes, my proficiency has come through repeated practical application, and yes, I present the subjects through the lens of my own experience in using them, as well as teaching them to others. The practical foundation on which all of this is built was gained in person from teachers and mentors. In particular, I would mention Juha Rankinen, from whom I learned much. Added to this was my study of the woodcraft techniques of old as laid out by Ernest Thompson Seton and Bernard Sterling Mason in particular. The content of Mors Kochanski's *Bushcraft* has also been highly influential. I gained much insight from the clarity of presentation of traditional subjects displayed by Ray Mears, initially from viewing his television shows, then from working with him in person. Working with Lars Fält provided me with a unique insight into the ways of the boreal forest, which I have built on in all of my subsequent winter escapades in the North. In this context I also thank my good friend and colleague Iain Gair, without whose enthusiasm for visiting the boreal forest I would not have had as many adventures there, nor as much insight into some of the subjects presented here. My ability to move through a wilderness by canoe is due to Ray Goodwin. Ray was my canoe instructor, but later we teamed up to undertake many wilderness canoe journeys. The experience of the wilderness on these trips has also been a massive influence on how many of the subjects in this book are framed. I also give thanks to all my colleagues over the years from whom I have learned something of woodcraft. There are too many to be named here. Similarly, I credit all the students who have asked questions, posed problems, needed coaching, and made suggestions. The feedback mechanism provided by this is woven intrinsically into everything presented here.

So *Wilderness Axe Skills and Campcraft* is a practical book about skills I use—some very often, others infrequently. There are a few variables that determine the space in which we are operating—(1) the tools, (2) the setting (woods), (3) the materials, and (4) the context (wilderness journeys and expedition-style camps). In reading the book, I'd like you to keep in mind the difference between what it is to be artisan and what it is to be practical, and when it behooves the . practitioner to be pragmatic and where there is space to move toward virtuosity, if desired. Throughout the work, safety and efficiency are principles that are never overruled or ignored.

A core principle here is the aim, or need, to get by with minimal tools, possibly because we are itinerant. We are not homesteading, nor are we running a workshop, inside or out. I am not a green woodworker in the traditional bodger sense, nor were any of my mentors (bodger is an old English term for a skilled itinerant woodturner who works with unseasoned wood). I come to these subjects via a lineage of bushcraft and wilderness-living-skills instructors and my own personal experience of undertaking wilderness trips through the seasons. This perspective is ingrained in the presentation of everything in these pages.

The reason I look older in some photos and younger in others is that the photos in this book were taken over the course of more than a decade. It should also be noted that I've used a fair amount of photos of students from my courses and of assistants who have helped me deliver those courses. This is partly because I like photography, and it's straightforward for me to capture images while I'm supervising students, or when my assistants are leading a session. Many of the photos in this book were not taken specifically with this book in mind. As such, some of the photos are maybe a little messy, with jobs half finished or seemingly incongruous items in the background. But it also shows these techniques are accessible. While it's true there is a difference between knowing a technique and being skilled in it, it's my view that it doesn't take years and years to become solidly proficient in most of what's in this book. While all of the techniques benefit from experience and some should definitely be turned into real skills over time to get the most out of them, I'd also encourage people to go out and get started with what they want to learn.

Most important to me is that what you find in this book is useful to you and that you will go out and apply it. It's important to keep alive the skills and knowledge of bushcraft and wilderness living. In an era of large-scale manufacture and consumerism, there is something rewarding in making things for yourself from natural materials. In fact, it seems to me there has always been a reward—both a practical physical reward coming from the object's utility, but also a psychological reward that comes from being able to create something of meaning. Crafting items from natural materials you find and harvest remains deeply satisfying and is possibly even more important now, from a psychological perspective, than it ever was before.

Entering the woods with a few well-chosen tools facilitates a great number of opportunities for fashioning useful items from natural materials. With knowledge of the materials available, and suitable techniques and skills derived from practice, you can make the things you want and need in the forest. These skills are enabling and give you freedom. You can make what you need when you need it.

Previous page: Friends of the author bringing firewood into camp on a winter hot-tenting trip in northern Sweden. Felling, sectioning, and splitting dead-standing timber such as this are made possible by an axe and a saw.

Right: Students working together on a Frontier Bushcraft course, applying various techniques learned in recent days.

Selecting the Correct Tools for the Job

Understanding Types of Axe

Axes are an iconic tool of woodcraft, featuring everywhere from the covers of old woodcraft and camping manuals to the logos of current outdoor-training companies. Even though the axe has largely been superseded by the chainsaw in professional forestry, axes remain popular among outdoor people as useful tools for camp and on the trail. Even general-purpose axes display a remarkable variety. Moreover, there are a number of more-specialist axe designs that remain relevant to woodland camps and wilderness huts or cabins.

Axe Anatomy

Before we look at different types of axes, it's worth reviewing some of the common terms used for parts of an axe.

Axe Handle

1. Axe head (see separate image for more detail)
2. Shoulder
3. Back
4. Belly
5. Throat
6. Grip
7. Lanyard hole
8. Swell or knob. This helps prevent your hand from slipping off the end of the handle. Traditionally, a highly ergonomic fawn's-foot or deer's-foot shape finished a general axe handle, particularly for a larger axe. Modern manufacturing techniques mean that the end of the handle is squared off perpendicular to the axis of the handle.

Axe Head

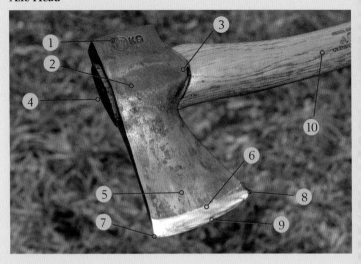

1. Poll or butt
2. Cheek
3. Lip or lug
4. Eye
5. Bit
6. Bevel
7. Toe
8. Heel
9. Edge
10. Handle, helve or haft (see separate image for more detail)

Axe Eye

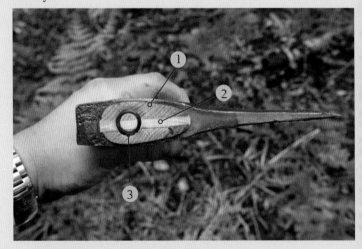

1. The handle. This single piece of wood comes all the way through the head apart from a slot cut into the middle to accept the wedge.

2. The wedge. A wedge is hammered into the end of the handle to fix the head into position. This is cut off flush with the end of the handle.
3. Staple. On some axes a metal staple of some kind is inserted to further fix together the wedge and the handle. Some manufacturers claim a staple makes no difference if the axe head is fitted correctly in the first place. Some users complain a metal staple makes it harder to rehandle the axe.

General-Purpose Designs

General-purpose axes are well suited to wilderness journeys and a variety of tasks around camp. The range of general-purpose axes available is largely centered on a core functional design, then scaled to purpose.

Despite the decline of the axe as a professional forestry tool, a small number of manufacturers continue to produce traditional axes. The axes that are worth seeking out have high-quality forged-steel axe heads and resilient hickory handles. The fashion in the last twenty years of traditional forest axes has been to go back to basics in terms of finish. There is no paint on the axe heads, and the raw wood of the handles is finished with either linseed oil or a mixture of linseed oil and beeswax, preserving a view of the wood grain.

General-purpose forest axes typically have a small poll, relatively little metal at either side of the eye, and a gently tapering concavity to the cross section of the bit as it approaches the bevel, which is usually convex. A convex bevel lends strength toward the cutting edge of an otherwise slender and elegant axe head cross section. A curved cutting edge is more efficient on green wood and typical

on forest axes of all sizes. Compare this to specialist carpentry axes meant only for seasoned wood; they have very straight edges. The handles of forest axes are not straight but, again, display gentle curves that lend themselves to the ergonomics and strong purpose of these workhorses. The handles are smooth, especially on the larger models. This allows the user's hand to smoothly transition from a position near to the head to a position near to the grip without too much friction.

In the context of popular axes on the market today, we can split the general-purpose axes into four size categories. These are a hatchet, half-length axe (or half axe), three-quarter-length axe (or three-quarter axe), and full-size, or felling, axe. All of them have general-purpose head profiles and together form a distinct category separate from more-specialist axes dedicated to splitting or carving, for example.

Most general-purpose axes have a slightly curved cutting edge.

The cross-sectional profile of general-purpose forest axes is quite slim, with the slope from the eye to the edge being gently concave except the final stretch down the convex bevel.

The hatchet is light with a short handle.

The half axe is a versatile and portable general-purpose axe but still quite short in the handle.

The three-quarter axe has a heavier head than the half axe and a handle about the length of my arm.

This felling axe, with a yet larger and heavier head plus a handle coming most of the way from my fingers to my sternum, is about twice as heavy as the three-quarter axe.

Hatchets

Hatchets are the classic small camp axe.

Hatchets are the smallest of the general-purpose axes. Being compact and relatively lightweight, they are highly portable. Hatchets are used one-handed. Compared to using a knife, hatchets make numerous light tasks around camp quicker or more efficient—or both; for example, fashioning wooden tent pegs or splitting kindling. Hatchets serve as good general axes for youngsters, in a comparable way as a larger axe serves as a general axe for an adult. For those who find their arm tiring quickly, or their wrist straining, while carving with a heavier axe, then switching to a hatchet could be the answer.

Typical measurements for a hatchet are a handle length in the region of 13½–15 in. (34–38 cm), with a total weight of 1¹/₃ –1¾ lbs. (0.6–0.8 kg)

Even among hatchets there is variation. The hatchet at the top of the image is smaller and lighter than the model at the bottom, which also has a more curved bit at the cutting edge.

The half axe is highly portable and a jack-of-all-trades.

Half Axes

Compared to a hatchet, a half axe has both a longer handle and a larger, heavier head. This gives the half axe both more overall weight and increased leverage. Sized against an adult with their arm held horizontally to their side, the handle of this size axe is equal to approximately half the distance from fingers to breastbone.

A half axe is just long enough in the handle to be swung two-handed, but also compact enough to be used one-handed. In addition to the general camp duties of the small axe, these axes can be applied to more-demanding jobs such as splitting heavier firewood and even felling trees.

Typical measurements for a half axe are a total length in the region of 19–20 in. (50 cm) with a total weight of 2–2½ lbs. (0.9–1.2 kg)

This makes the half axe easy to pack. Combined with a relatively low weight for an axe, the half axe is eminently portable. The size, weight, and design of the half axe present a versatile and portable general-purpose axe that suits many who try it. Personally, if I want an axe on a trip but don't feel I need something more specialized, the half axe is my default choice. It's a jack-of-all-trades that lends itself to any job I want to do, even if it is not optimized for any one particular task.

A half axe being used two-handed to fell a tree.

With the right technique, half axes can make short work of splitting firewood in camp.

Three-Quarter Axes

A three-quarter axe is an ideal light forestry axe. With a head at least as heavy as a half axe—often heavier—and a handle stretching roughly three-quarters of the way from fingertips to sternum of an adult, a three-quarter axe has greater momentum and leverage than a half axe. Their length and momentum means they are excellent for taking the branches off felled trees. Swung with the head low to the ground, the handle length means this size of axe is perfect for the job of limbing, also called snedding. Swung horizontally, the three-quarter axe is a surprisingly capable lightweight felling axe, a lighter and more portable option than a full-size felling axe. Three-quarter axes have significantly more chopping power than their smaller brethren due to the increased head weight and greater

handle length yet are still only a little more than half the overall weight of their full-size big brothers.

What you gain in some areas, though, you lose in others. For carving, the handle length of the three-quarter axe makes these axes a little too unwieldy. The same goes for some everyday camp axe techniques for splitting small kindling. The three-quarter length makes this axe somewhat awkward for small-scale jobs.

Typical measurements for a three-quarter axe are a total length in the region of 25 in. (64 cm), with a total weight of around $2^2/_3$ lbs. (1.2 kg).

Full-Size Axes

Full-size axes hark back to the old days of forestry, when felling was done by hand. This type of axe starts around twice the weight of a three-quarter axe, largely down to a heavier head, with greater edge length. These are designed for larger felling and are typically only used two-handed. They are very good for sectioning logs by hand too, making fast work of this task.

In terms of limbing, the full-size axe works well on larger branches, but the three-quarter axes are faster for removing multiple smaller branches since they have less inertia and can be accelerated with less effort. Full-size axes are also useful for splitting on chopping

The three-quarter axe isn't much bigger or heavier than the half axe, but it behaves more like a felling axe than a camp axe.

Selecting the Correct Tools for the Job

blocks around camps and cabins. They are worth considering for winter travel, although I prefer the greater versatility of the three-quarter axe. Full-size axes are too large for small splitting and carving. With a 3²/₃ lb. (1.5 kg) head, and a handle coming most of the way from my fingers to my sternum, my felling axe is about twice as heavy as the three-quarter axe.

A matter of scale. Three similar axes of different size, from left to right: felling axe, three-quarter axe, and half axe.

Typical measurements for a full-size axe are a total length in the region of 32–35½ in. (81–90 cm), with a total weight of around 4⁷/₈ lbs. (2.2 kg).

Specialist Designs
Splitting Axes

A thoroughbred splitting axe.

Splitting axes are designed to split. They are not general-purpose axes. They are not for felling. They are not for carving. They split wood. The design features mean that a good splitting axe works effectively and with brutal efficiency. Splitting axes are not a subtle tool.

The heads of splitting axes are wedge shaped and heavy. Looking at a splitting axe head end-on, you'll see it has more width across the eye than a general-purpose axe. This does two things: first, it puts a lot more metal into the head than a general axe, which

The head of a splitting axe versus a general axe of otherwise broadly the same dimensions. The splitting axe is much heavier and more wedge shaped.

increases its weight; second, it means the taper down to the cutting edge is more dramatic than a general axe. This makes it more of a wedge.

The handles of splitting axes tend to be a little less S shaped than forest axes, with a less pronounced belly. But they still have a swell that is ergonomically suited to the bit being edge down. Compare this to the splitting maul described in the next section. The grip of the handle on some models of splitting axes is knurled to aid your physical hold on the handle. The assumption is that you are going to be hitting hard with an axe like this, and your hands may become sweaty too.

The splitting axe on the left has pretty much the same handle length as the three-quarter axe on the right, and the head profile is a similar size. But the head of the splitting axe weighs 3.5 lbs. (1.6 kg), compared to the head of the general axe, which weighs 2 lbs. (0.9 kg).

For an axe with a heavy head, at first you might be surprised at how short a distance the edge has from heel to toe. This actually provides some advantage when the axe penetrates a round of wood but does not split it. It's far easier to remove an embedded splitting axe with a short edge from the wood than an axe with a longer cutting edge. Because the head is quite compact in this respect yet will be splitting rounds of wood with a diameter many multiples of this heel-toe distance, some manufacturers add additional protection to their wooden handles in the form of a

Chopper1® splitting axe with mechanical levers to help prize the wood apart.

Metal collar on a splitting axe.

metal collar. This prevents fibers from large lumps of wood from abrading the undersurface of the handle as the axe head passes through the wood.

From time to time you might also come across more-curious splitting-axe designs, such as the Chopper1®. The cutting edge of this axe is a similar length to a general-purpose forest axe of a comparable size, although the bevel is less broad and more steeply angled. What lies above this in the axe head is very different from most axes. There is a pair of rotating levers that are activated by the upper surface of the wood round and force the two sides of the wood apart. If you are splitting a very large round of wood, this axe works best if you split the sides off and work inward, rather than trying to split the round straight down the middle. There are other levered designs out there too, and it's always interesting to see what you might find in the woodshed of a wilderness hut or cabin.

The splitter with prizing levers (left) is a similar size to a large general-purpose axe.

Splitting Mauls

A splitting maul is a splitting axe with some special features. A maul has the same wedge-shaped bit as a regular splitting axe. A maul, though, is designed for use in conjunction with metal splitting wedges, as well as being used on its own as a splitting axe. The poll of a splitting maul is enlarged and the metal is hardened to withstand impact with other metal objects. The poll of a splitting maul is more reminiscent of a lump hammer than a regular axe poll. The poll of a maul can, therefore, also be struck with a hammer without risk of the damage that would otherwise occur.

If you hit metal splitting wedges, or other axe polls, with the poll of your regular axe, you will damage your axe. Other things being equal, the larger poll of a maul provides the advantage of more weight to the head too.

The other notable difference between a splitting axe and a splitting maul is the shape of the handle. A splitting maul has a straight handle. A maul is designed for use with the cutting edge down, as an axe, or with the poll down, as a hammer. The straight handle allows equal application as either.

Above: A splitting maul with a 5½ lb. (2.5 kg) head and a 31 in. (79 cm) handle.

The poll of a splitting maul is shaped and hardened to be a hammer.

End-on head profile of a splitting maul.

Choosing an Axe Fit for Purpose

Once you have an understanding of the types of axe available, the first question to ask is, What type of axe do you need? I use the word "*need*" over the word "*want*" intentionally. If you are buying your first axe, maybe a rational choice would be a general-purpose half axe. This would make sense for many people. Even if you amass an axe collection, you have to make choices. For example, what if your buddy invites you on a winter camping trip? You'll be walking on snowshoes and hauling toboggans. Are you going to take your entire axe collection? You have to make a choice about which axes you are going to take with you. And it needs to be a sensible choice based on the parameters of the trip. These parameters include weight of the axe, function of the axe, weight of other gear, weight of food, packing space, your fitness level, number and type of axes brought by other members of the group, how much firewood will be needed, how many hours of daylight will be available to process the wood, and how many people are in the group (division of labor is a real thing in the wilderness too).

When I undertake a canoe trip in Canada, I tend to take a half axe. It packs easily and does not add too much weight on the portages, yet it provides me with significant extra utility beyond a belt knife. Yes, I can baton wood with my knife, but I can split the same wood much more quickly with an axe. The axe also allows me to access firewood that a knife simply could not tackle, both in terms of splitting through knots as well as absolute size. With the axe I can clear off side branches quickly. If necessary I can remove dangerous trees from near where I need to camp, and I can clear a blocked portage trail that would otherwise impede my progress. I can fashion items for my camp quickly too. The half axe earns its place in my pack through its function combined with the demands and potential demands of the trip. I also see the argument for taking a three-quarter axe over a half axe on such trips, especially if you are out in the spring or in early fall, when it's going to be cold, particularly at night. You'll need more firewood for warmth, and there are shorter daylight hours to get everything done. I tend to do my trips in Canada when it's warmer than this latter scenario.

The author, along with his three-quarter axe, on a boreal forest hot-tenting trip.

Winter camping in the boreal forest, whether it be in the north of Scandinavia, in Canada, or elsewhere, is a different matter, even if I am traveling and camping in very similar locations to where I might canoe trip in summer. In terms of winter journeying, a three-quarter axe is my first choice for winter trips in the boreal forest. In this great northern forest of largely pine, spruce, and birch, an axe is the most important cutting tool. Yes, a saw is more efficient for cutting across the grain, but you can do everything you need to with only an axe. I'm not saying don't carry a saw as well as an axe. I'm purely stating the hierarchy of tools as it is apparent to me.

In winter a larger axe than the half axe has specific advantages. You need plenty of fuel on any winter trip in a forest, whether you're bivvying out or sleeping in a heated tent with a stove. Obtaining firewood in the boreal forest typically means felling dead standing trees, and then, of course, you have to process them. You have to remove branches, you need to section the trunks, and you need to split the wood into pieces that you can put into your stove.

The trees in the boreal forest grow more slowly than farther south, since the growing season is shorter. This makes the rings of the tree closer together, which makes the wood tougher. In turn, this means you need more cutting power from your axe than you do farther south.

In the boreal forest in winter, a larger axe has significant advantages. The objective choice is to take at least a three-quarter axe (as on the right, over the popular half axe on the left).

In my opinion, you need at least a three-quarter axe for boreal winter travel and winter camping. The additional handle length provides significant leverage. Also it has a heavier head and a slightly larger cutting edge than the smaller axes. This all being said, this size of axe can also be used for splitting wood around camp, and while they are a little too long in the handle for carving spoons and other utensils, they can be used one-handed for splitting smaller firewood. If there are a few of you on the trip, an option might be to have at least one half axe with you for smaller jobs around camp.

Despite the extra weight and size over a half axe, a three-quarter axe is still very portable, particularly if you think about the means by which you're going to be traveling in a winter environment. Some go further and specify a full-size axe for winter travel. I can see the reasoning, and I would not be unhappy to have a full-size axe with me on a winter trip. It's just that my three-quarter axe weighs half as much and gives me the utility I need on such a trip. A happy medium, which also has a lot of merit, is a three-quarter

axe with a heavier head than typical three-quarter axes. This keeps the form factor of the three-quarter axe but gives it more weight to cut through the tight-grained wood.

So, while we can be as objective as possible, some of our specification also comes down to personal preference, having tried a number of options. Whichever larger-axe option you choose for winter adventures, traveling by snowshoe with a toboggan, by snow machine, or by dogsled all allow easily taking a larger axe.

A full-size axe comes into its own for larger felling jobs or lots of sectioning. This is not something many people do in the chainsaw age. Felling axes are lovely tools to use, though, and certainly bring a smile to the face of axe enthusiasts. They require you to slow down and take advantage of the weight behind them. Reverting to a half axe after their use feels like becoming a little woodpecker. Felling axes also make a better splitting axe than lighter general-purpose axes, due to their increased head size and weight.

I have several splitting axes and mauls of different sizes and they make short work of large amounts of firewood splitting, which personally I find both fun and good exercise. To my mind, though, these specialist axes make the most sense in the context of feeding woodburning stoves on homesteads or in wilderness cabins. While I

Both a half-length and three-quarter length axe providing versatility to a winter hot-tenting group of multiple people.

enjoy using them in the forest, frankly I just don't need that much firewood in camp to justify bringing one for the job. I can produce all the split wood I need in a temporary base camp with a general-purpose axe.

Splitting axes are great for breaking down significant amounts of larger rounds of wood efficiently. (Photo by Martin Tomlinson).

A splitting axe with a fiberglass-reinforced plastic handle being used in a remote fixed camp in Canada.

Splitting axes can make sense in permanent camps though, especially when there are buildings or frame tents with stoves. In this case, you then need to consider whether a wooden-handled model makes the most sense, or whether a modern fiberglass-reinforced plastic-handled splitter is for you. The latter type is relatively inexpensive and requires little care, whereas wood handles need some maintenance to stay in good condition and don't fare well when left outdoors for prolonged periods. So which splitting axe you go for—traditional or modern—depends on the situation of your camp or cabin and who is going to be using the axe.

Remember, there are multiple manufacturers of axes. While they tend to make similar models, there is variation in detail from one manufacturer to the next. Some have heavier heads for a given size. Some have straighter handles. Some have broader heads. Some have more-curved cutting edges. Some splitting axes and mauls have concave wedge-shaped heads, while others are somewhat convex. There are, as with anything, different price points. Shop around and try things out if you can.

Important Observations When Choosing an Axe
Head Alignment and Attachment

Is the head on straight? Look down the edge of the axe to make sure it is aligned with the axis of the handle it is attached to.

Good alignment between head and handle.

Selecting the Correct Tools for the Job

Is the head firmly attached? Clearly, it goes without saying the head of any new axe should be rock solid in its attachment to the handle, with no play. But if you are picking up a used axe, even if it has been lightly used, it's certainly worth checking for any signs of movement. You can do this by feeling if the head is moving relative to the handle, but also by looking at where the two meet. If the head of an axe has moved on the handle, there will often be some sort of line or mark to show where it was before.

Grain Alignment

Is the handle grain aligned along its longitudinal axis? Look to see if the grain of the wood is along the handle or at an angle, cutting across it. With hickory handles, this is less critical than, say, with ash. Even so, if you have the choice between a handle with aligned grain and nonaligned grain, take the former over the latter. Grain that is aligned provides greater resilience in the handle than otherwise.

Here is a good example of the wood grain being perfectly aligned with the longitudinal axis of the handle, providing greater resilience.

Metal Staple?

With three-quarter axes and larger, where the impact forces at work are much higher than for smaller axes, some like to see an additional measure in ensuring the wedge does not move relative to the handle—that's some form of metal staple locking itself and the wedge in place relative to the handle.

Fit and Finish

To an extent, fit and finish is an aesthetic choice, but a well-finished tool also tends to demonstrate extra care in making it. This being said, handmade and hand-finished tools also tend to attract a higher price tag. So this consideration is also one of budget. Some areas of finish can be improved by your own efforts too. Many traditionally styled axes come with a raw wooden handle finished with a mixture of linseed oil and beeswax. Others come with a varnished handle. Yet others are painted. Some people have a strong preference for one versus the other. There seems to be a similar debate regarding oiled versus varnished in the axe world as there is about the pros and cons of these finishes on canoe paddles. One observation I would make is that varnish tends to be more impervious to moisture, but it's a pain to refinish if the varnish gets chipped. By contrast, oil is easier to maintain a smooth finish without the potential for chipping, but unless you have built up a lot of layers of polymerized oil on your axe handle, oiled handles are somewhat prone to the wood grain swelling as it takes on atmospheric moisture. So again, it's about specifying the conditions in which you need the axe to function in a particular way, alongside your personal preferences.

A Key Distinction

If you are based in a camp, not moving all your gear each day, then you generally have the luxury of having more kit with you. It's really nice to set up a good base camp and have a few luxuries such as cast-iron Dutch ovens for cooking great meals over the fire, as well as having the luxury of time to spend exploring the woods and carving interesting bits of wood you find when out and about. It's a matter of intention. I spend a good amount of the year living outside like this, running courses out of a temporary base camp in the woods. When I'm running a woodcraft course, then I will have many axes more than usual with me, most of which are for the students to use, try out, compare, and contrast. Ultimately, what you take with you is about the aims of the trip to the woods.

The above scenarios in a fixed camp are distinct from the relatively spartan existence of a self-powered wilderness journey. If you are making a journey, you generally have to choose one axe at most, sometimes less, to take with you. This comes down to considering the parameters of the journey and choosing a tool that allows you to undertake the likely tasks on this journey, as well as fit within size and weight constraints. Wherever you take your axe or use it, near or far, remember to enjoy the woods, respect the trees, and use your axe safely. Much of this book is dedicated to these ends.

Choosing and Using a Saw

Saws have specific advantages. Saws are more efficient in cutting across the grain of wood than a knife or an axe, both in terms of physical effort as well as amount of wood wasted. Saws are also far safer to use. I like to pair my belt knife with a small folding saw. Similarly, it makes sense to pair a general-purpose axe with a suitably sized saw. Knives and axes work very well along the grain, in carving or splitting wood. Having a companion saw to work across the grain provides you with the best of both worlds. Being able to saw off wood squarely has a number of benefits, not least being able to stand rounds of firewood on a chopping block.

Small Folding Saws

A folding pruning saw lends itself very well to woodcraft.

These teeth cut when pulled toward the user (to the right).

I carry a folding pruning saw along with my belt knife when I am in the woods and on wilderness journeys. This type of saw is usually designed to cut on the pull stroke. This is because there is no frame holding the blade taut. Cutting on the pull stroke means the blade is under tension, therefore straighter than on the push stroke. I like a small saw that is not going to break easily. If pinched in the cut, saw blades in Bahco Laplander saws tend to bend rather than snap. These can be bent back into shape. This is advantageous on remote trips where replacement is impossible. Robustness and reliability

are imperative. A further desirable feature is a locking blade, especially one that locks shut as well as open.

Camp Saws

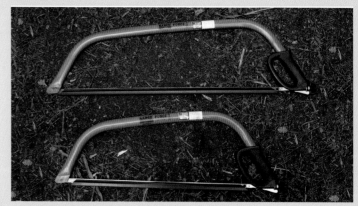

A pair of bow saws.

A larger general-purpose saw for use in a fixed camp can be applied to processing dead, dry wood for firewood or cutting green wood for camp structures or carving projects. Bow saws with metal frames are inexpensive and robust. They last a long time and represent excellent value for money. Bow saws come in a variety of sizes. Bow saws with a 24 in. (60 cm) blade length make for a good camp saw.

Larger Saws—Types of Saw Blade

There are a number of types of blade available for larger saws such as bow saws and bucksaws. The two main types are blades made

A bow saw is useful around a fixed camp.

for seasoned wood only and blades made to cope with sawing green wood. Seasoned wood blades have regular teeth all along their length. These are designed for efficient cutting of wood with low moisture content. Blades designed for cutting green wood have special raker teeth interspersed among the regular teeth of the blade. These raker teeth clear the sticky sawdust, preventing the cut from clogging and reducing the chance of the blade sticking. This latter type of blade can be considered a general-purpose blade. As well as cutting green wood, it will also cut seasoned wood, just not quite as efficiently as a dedicated seasoned wood blade.

Top is a general-purpose blade that will cut green wood as well as seasoned wood. Note the raker teeth. Bottom is a blade for seasoned wood only.

Saws for Traveling

In terms of taking larger saws on journeys, bow saws are fine for vehicle-based trips, where the saw can be slotted down the side of other equipment in the boot of a 4×4, for example. For self-propelled journeys, however, where packing space may be at a greater premium, fold-down saws have an advantage. There are two broad types: wooden framed and metal framed.

Traditional wooden bucksaws are elegant in design and light in weight. These saws have two uprights and a central cross-member. The blade is tensioned by means of a windlass, an ancient mechanism where a lever is twisted in a piece of cord to shorten it. On loosening the windlass, the saw breaks down into its component parts. Packed away into a slipcase, the components have a much-smaller form factor than the assembled saw.

I particularly like a wooden bucksaw for winter camping trips, since the wooden frame is relatively warm in the hand due to lower thermal conductivity of wood than metal (even when you are

wearing gloves, metal will sap more heat). While plastic handles can reduce the conductivity of metal-framed saws, plastics become more brittle in cold conditions.

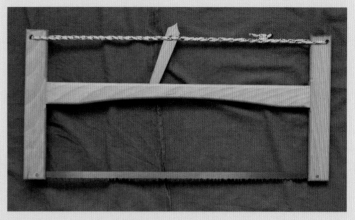

A traditional wooden bucksaw.

While I have used wooden-framed saws for canoe trips, there is a risk of them becoming saturated due to the canoe swamping or capsizing. Wood swells when wet, and this can cause the joints of a wooden bucksaw to become ill fitting. This is the primary reason I prefer a metal-framed folding saw for canoe trips. Metal-framed saws are also more robust and lend themselves to group use, where people may not take care of the saw as much as you would like. It is disappointing if your prized wooden bucksaw is scratched and chipped by inconsiderate users.

Axe and saw combination for winter camping.

Top: *the metal-framed saw folded down;* bottom: *the wooden-framed saw folded down.*

Top: *a metal-framed folding saw;* bottom: *a wooden-framed folding saw.*

Carrying Spare Saw Blades

You may wish to carry spare saw blades with you on a journey. This could be because your saw is fitted with one type of blade and you wish to have the option of fitting it with another type of blade. Or, it could be that you want a spare in case of breakage or wear. There are a number of neat ways of carrying spare saw blades. One is to cover the blade as supplied in its cardboard packaging with duct tape. Another is to purchase some Velcro® of sufficient width that it will envelop the blade and adhere above and below the blade as well as either side of it. The latter option is better for blades you want to have access to on a daily basis, especially if you want to swap types of blade in your saw. The duct tape option is adequate for keeping new replacement blades secure until you need them. Either of these options can be slipped into the case in which you keep your saw. Covering your spare blades means their sharp teeth do not damage other equipment, including the saw or its slipcase.

A couple of options for packing spare saw blades. Top: *duct tape,* bottom: *Velcro.*

Get a free how-to article on making your own folding bucksaw, including measurements and diagrams, at
wildernessaxekills.com/resources

Safe and Efficient Use of a Saw

Saws have far fewer safety concerns than axes. This being said, there are some basic safety principles we should follow with saws. These largely prevent cuts to the hand. Saws, particularly those with coarse teeth, can roam around on the surface of the wood before they properly bite and establish a defined cut. You don't want the saw to roam onto a finger or thumb. A simple way to avoid this is to reach across the saw blade, holding the wood to the other side of the saw blade.

The above reaching-across technique is the most failsafe for establishing cuts. Once the cut is established, you can move your hand back to a more orthodox position if you wish. This can include covering the cut with your thumb to help retain the blade. With smaller-diameter pieces of wood, you can leave your hand crossed over if you want to. With larger-diameter pieces of wood, though, it is important that you do remove your arm, since you will need the clearance between the blade and frame. For the more experienced user perhaps, particularly when you want to establish a cut in a very specific place, you can use your thumb as a guide. This is akin to how you might accurately establish a cut with a carpentry saw.

Reaching across a pruning saw.

Covering an established cut with the thumb. (Photo by Jeremy Ray).

Reaching through a bow saw to eliminate the chance of the blade roaming onto the hand. (Photo by Jeremy Ray).

Using the thumb as a guide while establishing a saw cut in a specific place.

To get the most from your saw, you should observe a few means of maximizing efficiency. First of all, use the full length of the blade, especially with bow saws and bucksaws. A common mistake is to saw with only the central portion of the blade. Another very common mistake I see with inexperienced saw users is they attempt to cut a piece of wood in between two points of support. As the cut deepens it will close onto the saw blade, pinching it and making the cutting effort much greater, or impossible. It is far better to position the wood so that gravity pulls part of the wood downward, away from the rest, thus opening the cut being created and freeing the saw blade rather than trapping it. Finally, if there are other people around, work together to secure the wood rather than struggling with an unwieldy piece of wood on your own. A companion can help feed the wood through to you for further cuts of firewood or collect the cut pieces as they are created.

By cutting beyond the points at which the wood is supported, the saw will not be pinched.

Cutting off the end of a sawhorse in a fixed camp also allows efficient cutting. Plus, a friend can both help stabilize the wood as well as feed it forward for the next cut.

Cut pieces of wood so the excess falls away and the cut is opened, freeing the blade.

Out in the wilds you can improvise and work together.

An Alternative Way of Using a Bow Saw

Saws work by their teeth moving relative to the wood being cut. The way most people imagine this to be done is by moving the saw and keeping the wood stationary. You can do the opposite, though. You can move the wood while keeping the saw stationary. This works well for sawing smaller-diameter wood quickly near a campfire while using a bow saw, especially if you have no sawhorse or other means to stabilize the wood.

1. *Place a thin but robust stick through the frame of a bow saw, then insert the end of the frame into soft ground, standing on the stick.*

2. *Holding the frame between your knees, the saw is now quite secure. Cut wood by moving it up and down the stationary saw blade.*

If you have a saw blade you can make a saw. You can make very similar designs to either a classic bucksaw or a classic bow saw, solely from materials found directly in the forest. Which design you make somewhat depends on the materials you have at hand, as well as whether you have access to an open fire.

Improvised Bucksaw

The first method is based on a design featured in Mors Kochanski's book *Bushcraft*. The species of wood you use will depend on where you are, but any straight hardwood or softwood stands a chance of working. More-flexible woods will lose tension more quickly than stiffer species of wood. The higher flexibility of some species may require larger-diameter pieces for the uprights than others. Like a workshop-made bucksaw, the improvised bucksaw has two uprights and a windlass for tensioning the blade. Rather than a jointed cross-member, a braced cross-member is created by joining two pieces of wood using either jam knots or constrictor knots.

To make the crosspiece, take two straight sections of wood, then chamfer them to fit together flat to flat at one end. This creates the fixed angle between the two pieces. Then they need to be lashed

A completed improvised bucksaw made using the Mors Kochanski method.

Wilderness Axe Skills and Campcraft 33

together. Mors's way is to use jam knots, but I have found that constrictor hitches bind down very well and don't slip laterally. This crosspiece needs to be sized correctly so the uprights are far enough apart to accommodate the saw blade you have chosen to use. Measure up against the saw blade.

There is a little bit of detail regarding the uprights. First, to aid stability of the structure, you should chamfer the inner surfaces a

This is a mistake made by a student. The constrictor hitches are sitting over a gap, not binding fully onto a surface. Later this will lead the knots to come loose and the saw to disintegrate.

Detail of the chamfered join between the two pieces making up the cross-member. Note also the flattening to the inside surface of the upright.

Create a slot in the base of each upright to accommodate the saw blade.

View from above of the constrictor hitches placed correctly.

little so the ends of the crosspiece sit on a flat surface rather than balancing on a curved one. Second, you must create a slot in the base of each upright to accommodate the saw blade. Ensure the slot is aligned correctly, at right angles to the flattened surface above. To create the slot, gently tap a belt knife into the end of the upright. The windlass is a piece of wood that acts as a lever, inserted into the string to twist it. The twisting increases the tension in the string, pulling the uprights together at the top and farther apart at the bottom. This latter action puts the saw blade under tension.

Windlass detail.

The second method is Kelly Harlton's H bucksaw. This is an evolution of the idea behind Mors Kochanski's method. Rather than having two cross-brace pieces and a single windlass, Kelly's H bucksaw has a single crosspiece and two windlasses. The original way the crosspiece was mated with the uprights was by creating a V notch in its ends and fitting this to squared-off sections of the uprights. A more recent simplification of the method is to create concave-curved ends to fit with the naturally rounded uprights. The latter is the way Kelly showed me in person. It seems to be easier for most people to achieve quickly and efficiently.

Detail of the mating between crosspiece and upright

A Harlton H bucksaw made by the author.

Improvised Bow Saw

This is a less universal technique than the improvised bucksaw, but nonetheless a useful one to know. You can make a wooden frame from one piece of wood if you have species with suitable properties available. I like to use hazel or willow for this.

The key is being able to find a staff of green material about 8 ft. (2.5 m) long with a reasonably consistent diameter, which should be around 7/8 in. (2 cm). You want to be able to create a smooth curve by bending the staff, so it's best if the staff is free of kinks and as free as possible of knots.

The bending is done with heat, over a low fire with embers. The area in the middle of the staff is heated to make it more malleable. This is gradually bent into shape, with the central section usually, although not always, forming the frame of the saw.

The central section of this staff is taking the shape of a bow saw.

Note the ends of the U-shaped piece of wood are tied off, and I am offering up a saw blade to determine where it will fit.

Once you have the central section of your staff bending and taking the shape of a bow saw, it's time to secure the ends of the staff. First tie them to each other loosely with some cord. Once tied off, you can allow the cord to take the strain. You should now make a final decision about which part of this U-shaped piece of wood the saw blade will span. Offer up the saw blade to the frame and picture where it will fit. Above this you will have to fit a temporary windlass, similar to what you would create for tensioning a bucksaw.

Attaching the windlass is a little tricky. If you don't use a suitable knot, it slips along the curve of the wood as you try to tension it. I have found using constrictor hitches works very well. Start with a constrictor hitch, then span above where the blade will fit to the other side of the wood. Attach the cord here also with a constrictor hitch. Then span back to where you started, finishing with a third

constrictor. Now you can pull the wood inward with the windlass. Note that the cord you use should be very strong. Paracord works well. Once you have windlassed some, taking the tension into the strong cord, the original cord at the ends of the elongated U will go slack. This is your sign to cut off the excess wood, since the shape will be maintained by the tension in the windlass.

Once you have cut away the excess, you are effectively left with the frame of your bow saw. Now you need to fit the blade. This is the same technique used to create the slots that accept the blade in the bucksaw. The difference is that you need to be careful not to cut the windlass string by accident. Once the slots are made, tap the saw blade into position. I usually use a nut and bolt at each end to retain the saw. You can also use nails, or small pieces of fence wire, anything that will hold the saw blade without being deformed by it. Once the saw blade is in position, you can release your windlass, letting some of the tension out of the wooden frame and pulling the blade taut and ready for action. The saw is now ready for use.

A completed improvised bow saw.

Knives for Carving

When it comes to basic whittling, almost any general-purpose blade designed for outdoor life can be used as long as it is sharp enough. There are, however, features of knives that mean they particularly lend themselves to woodcarving. Even some general-purpose knives are more suited to carving than others. Then there are also specialist woodcarving knives.

It makes sense for the woodcrafter to have, at least as a default, a general-purpose fixed-bladed knife suited to woodcarving as well as other outdoor jobs. If crafting with wood is going to be part of your repertoire, and, for reasons of weight or simplicity, you are going to pack only one knife, then good woodcarving functionality in your general knife is a must.

An alternative notion would be to carry a specialist carving knife in addition to a general-purpose knife, especially if the general knife is optimized to aspects of outdoor life other than woodcarving. If you are a hunter, you may want your general-purpose belt knife to be more optimized for skinning and butchery. Or you might desire your general-purpose knife to be highly robust for batoning or chopping, but it may then be too cumbersome for carving.

Ultimately, there is no universal right or wrong answer in terms of knife choice. It is a matter of personal preference combined with the parameters you are overlaying with respect to your time outdoors and the jobs you want the tools to perform. It's a case of being intentional in your choice and informed in your decision-making. To this end, following are some observations with respect to knives for woodcarving.

Blade Length, Weight, and Shape

For a general-purpose belt knife to be useful for woodcarving, there are a few aspects we should consider. First is blade length. You will see later in this section that specialist carving knives are actually quite short. So it is general-purpose blades that are useful in this respect. As a rule of thumb, look for a blade no longer than the width of your hand. Larger than this, they start to be somewhat unwieldy.

A general-purpose blade no longer than the width of your hand remains useful for woodcarving.

The increased size and weight of larger knives, such as the top two, may have benefits for some jobs, but for woodcarving, the bottom knife is preferable.

A knife is a three-dimensional object. We need to consider the thickness of the blade as well as its length. General-purpose knives, even those of a desirable length for woodcraft, vary significantly in thickness and, therefore, weight of the blade. Even though they are strong, blades above $5/32$ in. (4 mm) in thickness at the spine tend to be on the heavy side for woodcarving. Thinner blades with little or no flex tend to work well for woodcarving. In the context of a general-purpose blade, this means $7/64$ in. (2–3 mm) in thickness.

These blades are all a good length for a general-purpose woodcrafting knife but they vary in thickness from around 5/64 in. to 3/16 in. (2 mm to just over 4.5 mm).

The shape of a blade is an important determinant of its function. A flat bevel, or so-called Scandinavian grind, is well suited to woodcraft. Indeed, this is the preferred bevel shape on specialist woodcarving knives. As a principle this applies also to general-purpose knives. Moreover, in the context of a general-purpose outdoors knife, flat bevels are easy to sharpen in the field. In terms of the elevation profile of a blade, what also works well for woodcarving is gradual curvature of the edge to the point where the edge meets the back—and where they do meet, there is a fine point. Significant belly in the blade causes too rapid a change in edge angle for smooth carving cuts, as well as putting too much metal toward the tip of the blade for fine carving work.

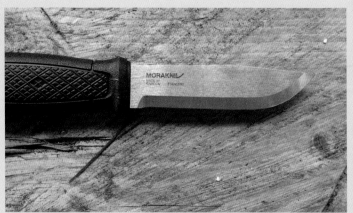

The top and bottom of this knife are parallel for quite a lot of its length, with a relatively sharp rise of the edge to meet the back. This shape has quite a lot of belly, and the point of the knife is not particularly fine, making it less of a woodcarving knife than other knives from the same manufacturer.

A companion knife designed by the author for general craftwork, including woodcarving .

We are not all the same size. A general-purpose knife that is a good size for me may be too chunky in the handle and too long in the blade for a smaller person. Moreover, shorter general-purpose knives, sometimes carried as a companion knife to a larger belt knife, can be very nice to carve with even for larger people.

This knife blade has a gradual curvature of the edge, rising to meet a slow descent of the back to form a relatively fine point toward the tip. Overall this is a general-purpose knife that has a shape that lends itself to woodcarving.

Specialist Carving Knives

If you are going to do a lot of woodcarving, it is worth considering purchasing a specialist woodcarving knife, distinct from any general-purpose knife you may be packing. This has the twin advantage of it being more efficient for woodcarving as well as removing some restrictions on the features of your general-purpose knife.

Specialist woodcarving knives tend to have relatively short, narrow, thin blades compared to even small general-purpose knives. Woodcarving knives often have handles with rotational symmetry so they can be held in a number of different grips equally comfortably. In this case the handles will feel the same with the knife in a forehand grip as in a reversed grip.

A short blade means cuts never put a large amount of leverage on the user's wrist. This means the carving cuts are very controlled, even when the cuts are made powerfully. This, combined with a very gradual, consistent curve, leads to these knives being capable of removing material from the workpiece with precision. Grip is maximized by putting a chunky handle on the knife despite it having only a small blade.

A specialist woodcarving knife from Mora. The blade is short, thin, and relatively narrow.

A specialist woodcarving knife by British maker Ben Orford. Note the thickness of the handle relative to the size of the blade.

Pairing a specialist carving knife with a spoon knife allows the user to carve many types of utensils and implements for use in camp.

Compare the woodcarving knife blades above to this robust general-purpose wilderness knife designed by the author, which is not optimized for carving.

Caring for Your Tools

How to Care for an Axe

A good axe of a traditional design has several components made of materials that require some maintenance. If you look after your axe, it will give you many years of service.

A good-quality traditional-style axe will likely have a wooden handle. As with any wood that is kept or used outdoors, it needs to have some protection from the elements, most notably water. When you buy a new axe, it comes with a protective finish on the handle. This finish is often made from linseed oil and beeswax.

A good axe will have a head made from high-quality steel. The head will be tempered so that the bit of the axe is tough, not easily

The difference between care and neglect. The two axes pictured here are the same model. At the time of the photo, the axe on the left was ten years old, well traveled, and well looked after. The axe on the right was one year old and had been left outdoors for all of that time, with no care given to maintaining it.

chipped, and able to attain a very sharp yet resilient edge. This high-quality piece of steel will also need some protection and care to keep it in prime condition.

The third component that we need to give some consideration is the mask, also commonly referred to as a sheath. A mask on a traditional-style axe typically will be made of leather. As with any leather item, it will need protecting from the environment to keep the leather in good condition.

Both of these axes have been well maintained.

How to Look After the Axe Head

Keeping your axe in prime working condition does, of course, include keeping it sharp. This is covered later in this chapter. What we're concerned with here is how to keep your axe in good condition and protected from the environment.

The head of a good-quality axe is typically made of steel that is not stainless. That is, it will quite easily rust if allowed to remain damp for a period of time. This would obviously have a detrimental effect on both the finish and, ultimately, the longevity of the axe head. So we must protect against moisture.

The easiest way to do this is to oil the axe head. Some oils are better for this than others. But in the absence of the ideal, anything is better than nothing. Personally I find that a gun oil, which is designed to dry once applied, is the best option. It remains on the axe longer. Also, since it dries quickly, it doesn't make the inside of the mask oily. Nor does it transfer onto other items of the kit while packed in a backpack. First remove the mask, then apply a thin layer of oil all over the metal of the axe head. Remove any excess with a cloth. Leave the oil to dry before refitting the mask.

How to Look After the Handle

The handle of a traditional-style axe will typically be made of wood; these days this will most likely be of good-quality hickory. Hickory is a very tough and resilient wood but will still last much longer with a protective finish.

We want to retain, if not improve, the finish that the axe handle comes with. While we can completely replace the factory finish on a wooden handle with a higher-quality finish, such as that traditionally used on gun stocks, this is not necessary for keeping the handle in good condition.

Maintaining the finish of a wooden handle is a case of simply applying a coat of boiled linseed oil from time to time. Please note that it must be boiled linseed oil, not raw linseed oil. Raw linseed oil will not dry easily and will remain sticky.

First make sure the handle is free of dirt, then simply apply the boiled linseed oil to the existing finish. To do this, use a small paintbrush to apply the liquid. Once you've coated the entire handle reasonably liberally, remove the excess with some paper towels. There should now be a thin layer of linseed oil left remaining on the handle. This can then be left to dry. This simple process provides another very fine layer of finish to the handle and increases its level of protection from the elements. Over time, if you keep adding single layers, you will build up a very good and resilient layer of finish on your axe handle.

How to Look After the Mask

If you have a mask that is made of leather, it will need to be cared for. You must remember that the mask is designed to protect you and your other equipment from the sharp edge of the axe bit. The mask must retain its original good fit. You do not want the mask to become loose or to fit sloppily. Therefore, you shouldn't apply any treatment that will soften or allow the leather to stretch beyond its original size and shape.

If you follow the above simple steps to look after your axe and apply them on a regular basis, your axe will stay in top condition for many years to come.

How to Sharpen an Axe

General-purpose axes have convex bevels. Even the wide, heavy heads of splitting axes are convex close to the edge. The benefit of a convex-bevel profile is a greater cross section of metal close to the edge than provided by a flat bevel. This makes the axe bit more robust and less likely to chip.

So it's important to preserve the bevel shape while also keeping your axe sharp. To maintain the bevel profile of your axe, you need to sharpen it in such a way as to not only remove metal at the edge, but remove metal evenly across the whole bevel. If you sharpen a convex bevel only closest to the cutting edge, you will soon create a secondary bevel. This is undesirable and to be avoided.

Sharpening stones and metal files are the tools of axe sharpening. These sharpening tools have flat surfaces. This means if you place the stone or file at any point on a convex bevel, it will be touching the bevel only tangentially at the point of contact. So to remove metal from the whole bevel, you need to vary the angle of the stone or file relative to the bevel.

A further issue with sharpening axes is that the cheek of the axe can impede the action of a sharpening stone. If you take a bench stone and rock it through the range of angles that it can touch the bevel, the far end of the stone will rise and fall quite significantly. As it falls, it can come into contact with the cheek of the axe, thus impeding sharpening angles beyond this. Hence, it is better to use a short, compact stone, which can complete the full range of angles required to abrade the bevel without

the angle being restricted by the stone coming into contact with other areas of the axe head.

So, if a short, compact sharpening stone is what we need to keep our axe keen, can we just use a pocket stone? This is something we are likely to have with us anyway as part of our basic outdoor outfit, along with a belt knife. While you can indeed use pocket slip stones to sharpen an axe, you do need to be very careful not to cut your fingers. These stones are very thin, so holding them necessarily means your fingertips protrude beyond their surface, potentially bringing them into contact with the edge of the axe. This is less likely if you use a small pocket stone in the same way you would use a file against an axe, but it doesn't make it impossible to cut yourself.

A thicker stone allows you to hold the stone with your fingers in such a way that they do not extend beyond the stone surface that is working the axe bevel. This means there is no chance of any of your fingertips coming into contact with the cutting edge.

Purpose-made axe stones are available. These tend to be rounded like a hockey puck. An alternative is to acquire a combination bench stone (which is also thick) and cut it in half. You then have a stone that is the length of many pocket slip stones but with the thickness of a larger stone, which helps protect your fingers. If I need to remove more-serious chips from the edge of an axe, I also carry a metal file. I work the axe with the file first, then move onto the stone once I have sufficiently reshaped the bit. In fact, you can get an axe remarkably sharp with just a file.

Purpose-made hockey-puck-style axe stones.

A combination waterstone cut in half makes a good axe stone.

A file for remedying chips and sharpening an axe.

As well as a convex bevel, most general-purpose axes have a curved bit, so you have curvature in two different planes. The upshot of this is that a circular-to-oval motion, with pressure being applied during the phase when the stone is moved toward the edge, is an efficient and fluid sharpening stroke.

Sharpening Steps

Start with the stone's coarse side, work along the edge, then work back from the edge across the bevel again, then back the other way at a shallower angle still. Repeat until metal has been removed from the whole bevel. Do this again a few times. Then swap to the opposite bevel, making the same number of passes. Keeping the work you do on both sides broadly symmetrical is important to avoid losing symmetry in the bevel profile.

Continue with the above methodology until the axe starts to feel sharp. Then switch to the fine side of your stone and repeat the whole process.

Like a knife, stropping can finish the sharpening process very nicely, but it's worthwhile only with better-quality steels. While you can strop on a leather belt, this feels clumsy even with half axes, not to mention larger axes. Better to take a strop to the axe. I do this with a homemade board strop or paddle strop created by gluing some leather onto a piece of board. You can use a small amount of metal polish as a stropping paste.

1. *Working the stone close to the edge of the bevel.*

2. *Working toward the back of the bevel to remove metal there. Note the apparent gap between the stone and the bit, caused by the convex curvature of the axe bevel.*

3. *Sharpening the opposite bevel. At first glance it looks like the same bevel in all three photos, but notice the axe is being held handle-up in the first photo.*

4. *Pushing a board strop over the edge with some metal polish as a stropping paste.*

5. *The finished article.*

1

2

4

5

Knife Sharpening

There is an old adage that you are only as sharp as your knife. A blunt knife is inefficient, and as it becomes more blunt, it becomes both increasingly ineffective as well as increasingly dangerous. Sharp knives are predictable. You know they will cut what you want them to. So, we need a methodology for keeping our knife, or knives, sharp both at home and in the field.

The aim of a practical sharpening method is for you to efficiently achieve a keen edge that is fit for purpose. At the very least, all you need is an inexpensive combination oilstone and an old leather belt. An alternative is a combination Japanese waterstone. Bench stones are generally used in the workshop or at home. Bench stones are quite heavy, and you would certainly not be sensible to hike with one in your backpack. On the trail you are going to be carrying maybe a pocket stone. The principles of sharpening are exactly the same, though, regardless of the stone. We'll examine the principles by using the oilstone as an example. Only the use of oil is specific to this type of stone. Otherwise the methodology carries over to other types of stone, such as waterstones.

Getting Started

Find a flat surface that won't be damaged by oil. If you are outdoors, a tree stump or chopping block is ideal. Place the stone with the coarse side up. Apply plenty of oil. Now you are ready to begin sharpening.

Apply plenty of oil to the coarse side of the sharpening stone.

Achieving the Correct Bevel Angle

All knives have bevels. A bevel is the part of the blade that angles down toward the cutting edge. A general-purpose knife is typically symmetrical and has a bevel on each side of the blade. You must remove metal from both bevels to form a fine edge where they meet. To achieve the correct bevel angle, place your knife flat on the stone, then tilt the knife toward the cutting edge until the bevel angle is flush with the stone.

1. *Place your knife flat on the sharpening stone.*

2. *Tilt the knife toward the cutting edge until the bevel is flush with the stone.*

Sharpening Action

Start with the knife on the end of the stone nearest to you. Holding the handle in the hand you would use the knife, and with the cutting edge facing away from you, tilt the knife until you achieve the correct bevel angle. You should apply pressure with your fingers toward the leading edge of the knife. Now gradually move the knife away from you along the stone.

The length of the knife blade is likely to be greater than the width of the stone. You will have to move the knife across the stone as you move it forward so that you cover the entire length of the knife.

You'll notice that as the blade curves up toward the tip that the bevel loses contact with the stone. To compensate for this, you should slightly lift the handle of the knife toward the end of the sharpening stroke. Doing this means the curved tip of the knife drops and comes into contact with the sharpening stone, maintaining the correct bevel angle. This takes a bit of practice to get exactly right.

Look at the bevel you have just passed along the stone. Where metal has been removed, it will show up as obvious scratches or shiny areas. If your technique is correct, you will see that metal has been removed from the whole bevel. If not, adjust the angles as necessary.

To sharpen the opposite bevel, you should turn the cutting edge to face you and place the knife on the end of the sharpening stone farthest away. Again, tilt the knife so that the bevel is flush with the stone.

1. *Apply pressure with your fingers and move the knife away from you along the oilstone.*

2. *Move the knife across the stone as you move it forward.*

3. *Lift the handle to maintain contact with the stone toward the tip of the knife.*

4. *Metal should have been removed evenly from the entire bevel.*

Then, this time using your thumbs to apply pressure, draw the knife along the stone toward you. As before, you will also need to gradually draw the knife across the stone and lift the handle toward the end of the stroke to take metal off the whole length of the bevel.

If you are new to this process, after several passes on one bevel check to make sure you are achieving the correct bevel angle throughout the sharpening strokes.

As you take metal off each bevel, you will create a very thin foil of metal where the bevels meet at the very edge. This is pushed one way and then the other as you alternate sharpening each side of the knife. Running your thumb down the bevel (i.e., not along the blade but across it), you can feel this catch a little on the ridges in your thumbprint. This is sometimes referred to as a burr or wire edge.

5. *Turn the knife so the edge is toward you, and run it along the stone from the far end, using your thumbs to apply pressure.*

6. *Maintain the bevel angle and an even pressure as you move the knife forward and across the stone.*

7. *Again, lift the handle to maintain the correct bevel angle toward the end of the stroke.*

8. *Regularly check you are achieving the correct bevel angle.*

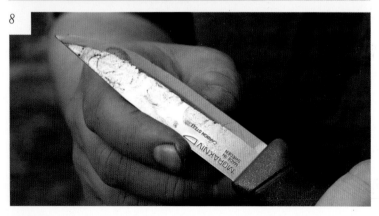

Sharpening Method

To ensure you are removing metal equally from both bevels, you need a sharpening method that keeps track of the number of times you pass each side of the knife over the stone.

The method should also take the knife to a progressively finer edge.

Here's a ten-step process that will do both:

1. Start with the coarse side of the stone up and apply oil.
2. Make eight strokes away from you.
3. Turn the knife and make eight strokes toward you.
4. Repeat steps 2 & 3 until the edge starts to feel like it has a burr.
5. Make one stroke away from you.
6. Make one stroke toward you.
7. Repeat steps 5 & 6 (i.e., alternating one stroke away, then one toward) ten to twenty times.
8. Swap to the finer side of the stone and apply oil.
9. Repeat steps 2 & 3 (i.e., eight strokes one way, then eight the other) three or four times.
10. Repeat steps 5 & 6 ten to twenty times.

The finish on your bevel should now be looking a lot finer, and the edge should be sharp.

Working on the finer side of the oilstone.

A smoother finish on the bevel after multiple passes on the finer side of the oilstone.

How to Check That Your Knife Is Sharp

If you have followed the steps above, then your knife should be sharp. It is, however, worth checking for any dull spots.

You can check this by carefully running your thumb across the edge (not along it) with no pressure. A sharp edge will catch the ridges of your thumbprint.

Carefully run your thumb across the edge to test if it is sharp.

You can also check visually. Orient yourself toward a light source and angle the knife to see if any light reflects off the edge. Any flat spots will reflect more light than a very sharp edge.

Look down the edge for any bright spots indicating blunt areas.

A 1000/6000 combination waterstone.

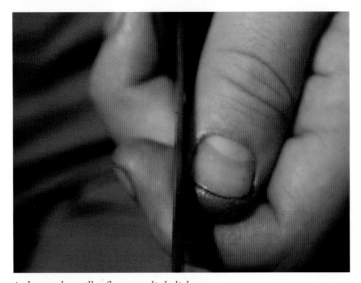
A sharp edge will reflect very little light.

Using Waterstones

The sharpening action and methodology described previously is exactly the same for bench waterstones. The major difference is that you don't use oil on waterstones; you use water. Just to be clear, you should never use oil on a waterstone. If you want to purchase one waterstone to sharpen your knives, then a combination stone of 1000/6000 grit is ideal.

You can sharpen your general-purpose belt knife on a waterstone. With the 6000-grit side of the waterstone, you will achieve a finer finish than with a typical hardware store oilstone. This is a

very good option for any specialist-woodcarving knives you may have. These knives also have flat bevels, so you can use the same methodology as described to sharpen them. You generally won't need to lift the handle as much or at all to maintain contact between the front of the blade and the stone. Moreover, if you feel that the carving knife needs to be worked on the 1000 grit to get it back to prime, flat-beveled condition, then by all means use it. I will use the coarse side from time to time, but often I just work the knife on the 6000-grit side, then strop it.

Working a woodcarving knife on a Japanese waterstone.

To Finish Off—Stropping

To smooth the edge and remove any remaining burr, you should strop your knife. For this we can use a leather belt, which many of us carry around our waists every day. If you don't want to use your best leather belt, then use an old one or purchase an inexpensive one for the job of stropping. Charity stores and military surplus stores are potential sources.

Attach the belt to a solid upright, such as a tree. Grip your knife in the hand you normally hold it in, and the belt in the other. To strop your blade, run it along the unfinished inside of the belt, leading with the back of the knife (i.e., with the sharp edge trailing).

The angle should be the same as or slightly above the angle of the bevel, so that you feel like you are slightly scraping the belt with any burr on the knife. Don't overdo lifting the angle, however, since you can round off the edge. As with the sharpening stone, make sure you move the blade across the strop as you move along it, so as to cover the whole length of the blade.

Alternate the stropping strokes away and toward yourself. Be mindful of the hand that is holding the belt on the strokes toward you. Fifty to one hundred strokes are usually enough.

Your knife should now feel razor sharp. A final test of its sharpness is to slice the edge off a sheet of paper.

1. *Stropping a knife on an old leather belt.*

2. *The away stroke, with sharp edge trailing. Note the angle is raised slightly above the bevel angle.*

3. *The stroke toward the body, again with sharp edge trailing. Remember to cover the full length of the blade.*

4. *Slicing the corner off a sheet of paper with a razor sharp blade.*

Get a free 60-minute video on knife sharpening at
wildernessaxekills.com/resources

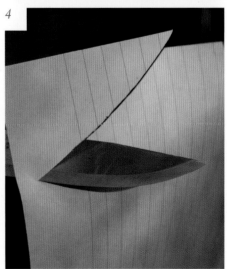

Board Strop

You can easily make, then use, a small board strop, somewhat like commercially available paddle strops. If you make it small enough, it'll be portable. Take an old piece of thick leather, such as from a leather jacket or leather chair, which has raw leather on the reverse. After cutting the leather to shape, glue the leather smooth side down (raw side up) to a piece of wood or fiberboard around ½ in. (1.25 cm) in thickness.

This type of strop can be used on its own, like the belt, but it can also be used with some form of stropping paste. While there are specialist stropping-paste formulas available, you can also use regular metal polish, which you may already have. I use an auto metal polish that is easily available. Place a small blob of the paste on your strop, then take the knife to the strop or the strop to the knife. I prefer the latter. I also use this same method for stropping an axe.

1. *Glue the leather to a piece of board to create your paddle strop.*

2. *Add a small amount of stropping paste or polish to your board strop.*

3. *Working the strop on the knife.*

4. *Having flipped the knife, now work the other bevel. Keep alternating for a few goes each side.*

5. *Clean off any remaining polish and assess the knife.*

6. *A sharp and shiny knife, ready for some woodcraft.*

Sharpening Spoon Knives and Other Curved Blades

The principle of sharpening a spoon knife is the same as sharpening a woodcarving knife. The issue we need to negotiate, though, is that the spoon knife blade is curved rather than dead straight. While we are looking at the spoon knife blade, we should also notice it has a bevel only on the outside of this curve. From the perspective of sharpening, this actually makes life a little easier than if the bevel were on the inside of the curve.

Similar to how you can easily make a board strop, here you can easily produce the sharpening tool you need. First you need a straight piece of wood that is rectangular in cross section, about ½ in. (1.25 cm) thick and 1 in. (2.5 cm) wide. Round off the edges on at least one side, then wrap some fine wet/dry sandpaper around the stick. I use P600-grade paper, and this works well. You need to secure the paper in place with glue, rubber bands, or string. Once this is done, you have the sharpening rod you need to sharpen spoon knives.

It's important that the sharpening rod is flat on one side, like a file, and rounded on the edge. For this reason, a piece of dowel is not what is needed, even though it would do half the job very well. You need both a curved surface and a flat surface on your sharpening rod.

1. *Straight pieces of wood rounded off on one or both sides, and some P600 wet/dry sandpaper.*

2. *The cross section of the wooden rod.*

3. *The completed sharpening rods.*

It's also worthwhile setting up a sharpening station where you are working on an improvised plinth, so you can achieve all the sharpening angles you want. Working on a flat surface such as a bench will not allow you to achieve some of the angles.

There will be two orientations in which you will be holding the spoon knife to sharpen it: one to access the inner part of the blade, and the other to access the outer surface, and specifically the single bevel. In each of these two orientations the sharpening rod is pushed toward the spoon knife.

4. *Set up a raised plinth that you can work on. Here it's a small log on top of a bench seat in a temporary camp.*

5. *The first orientation, to access the inner part of the curved blade with the sharpening rod.*

6. *The second orientation, to work on the outer part of the blade with the sharpening rod.*

7. *As you work the outside, beveled surface, you will see that you are taking metal from it consistently by the markings on the bevel.*

8. *Working the bevel on the outside will put a burr on the inside edge. This will need to be reduced or removed.*

9. *When you are working on the bevel, like when sharpening other knives, try to maintain the correct bevel angle, keeping the sharpening rod as flat to the bevel as possible.*

10. *Ensure you work the entire bevel from side to side, using the flat part of the sharpening rod.*

4

5

6

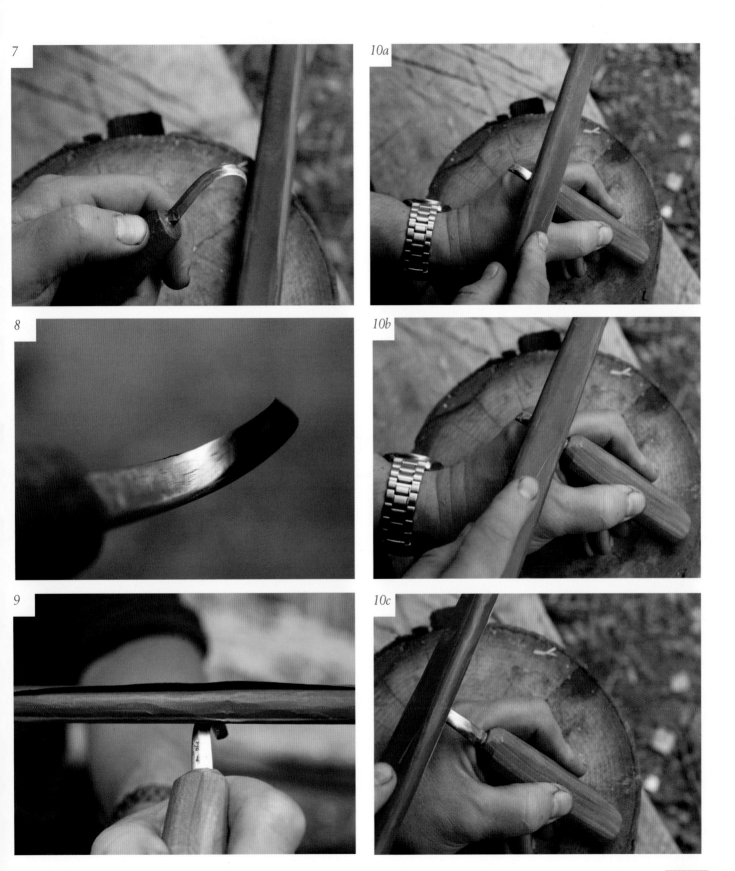

As with other sharpening work, alternate the sides you are working on and seek to reduce any burr. Then you can strop if you wish to (*see below*). You can follow a very similar sharpening process for many curved edges, such as gouges or adzes. You'll notice that the adze here has the bevel on the outside of the curve as well, which shouldn't be too surprising, since it does a similar job to the spoon knife but on a larger scale. Once it's sharpened, you can then strop the adze by using a board strop. You could use a board strop on the outer surface of the spoon knife but not the inner surface. What you could do, though, is employ a paddle strop of similar dimensions to the sharpening rod. The stropping process is then the same. Remember, you are pushing the strops over the sharp edge, not into it.

11. *Ensure you cover the whole of the inside surface of the blade, using the curved surface of the sharpening rod.*

12. *Pushing a board strop over the bevel of an adze.*

13. *First-person point of view of stropping an adze's curved blade.*

14. *The shine on the bevel probably speaks for itself, but this adze was a lot better after a quick sharpen-and-stropping session.*

11a

11b

Everyday
Axe
Techniques

Axe Safety Foundations

Safety in an outdoor activity, including using an axe, comes down to managing risk. Risk can be broken down into two components: likelihood and severity. While the likelihood of cutting yourself with your axe is similar to the likelihood of cutting yourself with your knife, the severity of axe wounds tends to be greater and, in the worst cases, very debilitating. An axe has more weight, more leverage, and more momentum than a knife. Moreover, when out camping or making a journey, we tend not to be wearing any sort of protective clothing or footwear. Our protection from injury with an axe has to come from care, attention, and good habits.

Adhering to best practice is particularly important in more-remote settings. Even a minor injury can cause problems on trips. Hygiene and the risk of infection are, of course, concerns. Loss of function is another. Axes can easily cause tendon, ligament, or nerve damage, particularly in your hands. A cut to a muscle causes swelling and pain, even if it still functions reasonably well. Not being able to grip a canoe paddle properly due to a cut on your hand or not being able to walk properly due to an injury on your leg are significant issues on a wilderness trip. If you are reliant on your own locomotion to power yourself through the wilds and back home again, it's incumbent on you to do your utmost to avoid injuries.

I'm a big proponent of training for the wilds even when you are close to home. The best way to ingrain good habits is to do them all the time, without exception. Practice makes permanent.

Throughout this book I highlight key safety points specific to particular techniques, but what follows is a general introduction to axe safety. You are most likely to be using axes in camp and in the direct vicinity of camp. This is where we should start.

Axe Safety Around Camp
Carrying Your Axe
When carrying your axe around camp, make sure the axe's mask is on. This is for your benefit and for the benefit of any companions. Modern axes by manufacturers producing the top-quality models have very good-quality steel axe heads. These are tough yet will hold a very sharp edge. Even brushing such a highly sharpened edge against clothing or skin will cause minor damage. The axe mask will help prevent damage to your clothing and equipment, as well as your skin, on a day-to-day basis.

A leather axe mask, however, won't protect you from the edge under all circumstances. I've seen people cut straight through the metal rivets of a leather mask by forgetting to remove the cover before tapping the axe into a chopping block. If you were to trip and fall onto the axe head, even with the mask on, you are likely to be badly injured. Hence, you should carry the axe in such a way that if you trip or slip and fall, then you will not fall directly onto the axe.

High-quality axe steel allows for robust yet very sharp cutting edges. Our good habits are the best protection from injury when using these excellent tools.

Carry your axe with the mask on. A straightforward safe and comfortable carry is to hold the handle directly below the head.

Carrying the axe in your hand allows you to easily jettison it if you fall.

Side view. This carry works particularly well for heavier axes, or those with longer handles.

Personally I don't like clipping the strap of the mask into my belt, as is suggested by some, even some axe manufacturers. Apart from the axe flapping around at my side, which is annoying, the security of the axe is entirely reliant on the pop fastener on the mask remaining closed, which gravity, combined with the mass of the axe, is conspiring against. Hanging the axe from the mask also stretches the mask strap, over time leading to the mask becoming too loose. Equally I don't like having an axe slipped into the slot some pants have on the side of the leg for this purpose. I don't want an axe attached to my leg if I slip or trip over. It also significantly impedes walking even short distances.

One somewhat unorthodox way I do sometimes temporarily store a half axe when I need to move around camp or a work area but keep my hands free is to slip the handle down the back of my belt, in between the belt and the pants. The head will then sit above the back of the belt. I only ever do this with the mask on the axe. I would also recommend that this doesn't become a habit for hiking around generally, to and fro, from camp to areas you might be working in the woods with the axe. If you slip over on an incline or are stepping on slippery bark on logs, for example, you'll possibly injure yourself by landing on the axe. Even in camp you should also seriously consider finding another carrying solution if the conditions you are moving around in are slippery, such as on rock or mud. If you slip over, a fall that might have otherwise meant only a bruised behind could be a lot worse if there is an axe between you and the ground.

Another well-balanced, relatively safe carry is to grasp the head behind the bit of the axe and cradle the handle in your elbow.

A student adopts one of the temporary axe storage solutions I like— down the back of the belt. See main text for caveats though.

Wilderness Axe Skills and Campcraft　61

At this rocky campsite in Ontario, Canada, my axe was placed off to the side, out of the way of other activities around the campfire.

Leaving Your Axe Unattended

You may know where you left your axe, but others will not. Leave your axe in such a way as to minimize people kicking, standing on, or otherwise coming into contact with your axe. Even if the mask is on, an axe can injure people if enough force is applied. Sometimes you need to leave your axe unmasked while you do something else for a short while, before returning to use the axe. The safest place for it is in a stump or a log, with none of the cutting edge exposed.

If you and your companions are working with multiple tools in the woods, then it's good to group them in a sensible place.

Taking a break from carving, this user has embedded their axe in the stump they were working on. None of the cutting edge is exposed, and the axe is in the block firmly enough that it won't easily fall out.

Often easier than introducing the axe to the end grain of the wood in the top of the stump is to put it into the side, where it is more aligned with the grain. This also leaves the top of the stump free.

Giving Yourself and Companions Enough Room

When setting up and organizing your camp, give some consideration to what you'll be doing with an axe in the area. Will you need to split firewood? Do you have a chopping block? What size of axe is being swung? Consider other camp activities, such as managing the campfire or food preparation and washing up, as well as routes to the water supply, latrine, and sleeping areas. You don't want someone swinging an axe too close to where others are working or in between areas they need to walk to and from, forcing them to walk past an active axe. Remember, it's not just the axe being used in situ that you need to think about, but also that the firewood being split can fly off the block. There is also the question of what if someone lets go of the axe by accident.

Where Does It Go Next?

This is a question you should always ask when using a cutting tool. What happens if I slip? What happens if it glances off? What happens if it cuts straight through what I'm working on? What happens if I miss? What happens if it bounces back? In each of these cases, where does it go next?

You never want the answer to the question of where it goes next to be part of your body. Especially when it comes to using an axe. Be deliberate, especially when learning how to use an axe, or if

During a winter camping trip in Sweden, a platform of snow has been trampled for the tent but has also been extended to be large enough to contain a firewood-processing area—in the foreground—that does not interfere with movement to, from, or around the tent.

you haven't used one for a while. To adopt the old saying, which is sometimes attributed to tailors and sometimes to carpenters, measure twice and cut once. This is a generally useful guideline in woodcraft but also specifically helps with safety by reducing the opportunity for impetuous action.

Aligning the axe with the grain of a log allows it to be easily placed in the log. Plus the handle is not sticking out sideways for anyone to trip over.

Dynamics of an Axe

Even general-purpose axes of a very similar design but different sizes behave differently to others. Different-length handles and different-weight heads impart a range of dynamics. A heavier head increases momentum, and a longer handle increases leverage. Where you hold the axe also alters the way the axe behaves.

1. *Think about the length of the axe you are using and which parts of you lie in the arc it will be traveling on when swung.*

2. *The half axe swings down to around my knee height.*

3. *The three-quarter axe heads toward my shin.*

4. *The felling axe heads toward my ankle.*

5. *As soon as I kneel with the half axe, the risk to my kneecap, or any of my leg for that matter, is greatly reduced.*

Working with a Camp Axe

Half axes have become very popular in recent years. As this book shows, they can be used one-handed or two-handed; can be turned to many tasks, from felling, to carving, to splitting kindling; and are highly portable. Even if you are using a larger axe for light forestry, you might well have a smaller axe in camp. Half axes make great camp axes.

The compact size of a half axe, however, means that you are often better off kneeling while using it, for better body mechanics as well as for safety reasons. This is especially the case when the block you are working on is quite low, as it often seems to be. Kneeling in front of a chopping block presents you with a few choices. The first choice is where on the block you should work.

1. *Working on the part of the block closest to you leaves less margin for error before you miss the block.*

2. *Working on the part of the block opposite your body puts a lot more wood between you and the axe.*

3. *If you are working one-handed on the block, particularly with a slicing motion when carving, it's good to position your body off to one side. This is ergonomically more comfortable, but also safer.*

4. *By offsetting your body to the block, any follow-through movement will not be toward you, but alongside you.*

Mind Those Fingers

If you are splitting on a block (*see opposite page*), then you can keep your hands well out of the way. If you are carving, though, you are going to have to keep hold of the workpiece, steady it, or move it while working on it with the axe. It's important then that you follow some rules to minimize risk of injury to the hand not holding the axe.

1. If you are carving, you have to keep hold of the piece you are working with the axe. A few safety rules will help protect your hand.

2. Act like your fingers have already been chopped off. Keep all your digits clear of the work you are doing. It's easy to hold the work with the palm of your hand, with fingers and thumb retracted.

3. The other important rule is not to raise the cutting edge of your axe higher than the hand that holds the work. This way you can never accidentally cut down onto your hand.

Firewood Splitting—Fundamental Techniques

In many situations, firewood is a daily requirement. Having a range of techniques to produce all the sizes you need from varied sources is fundamental. Context is also important. In a semipermanent camp setup, you are more likely to have a larger axe and a better chopping block. You may also be undertaking more-elaborate cooking. In contrast, on a wilderness journey you are more likely to be using small fires and cooking simpler meals. You are also less likely to have a large axe or a decent chopping block. Summer and winter also bring different requirements for warmth.

Splitting on a Block with a Larger Axe

Splitting firewood on a chopping block is one of the archetypal images that comes to mind when using an axe. This is something you are less likely to be doing on an overnight camp during an itinerant journey, but more likely to be doing in a temporary or semipermanent campsite, where you have gone to the trouble of sourcing a reasonably sized chopping block, as well as having the need for an ongoing supply of decent firewood. Even though this use of an axe is certainly familiar to many, at least in concept, there are still some subtleties to be understood to use the axe efficiently and safely.

First of all, the safety pointers for using an axe around camp, covered in the previous section, are assumed as read. In the context of using a block, one detail I will reiterate here is as follows. When you put your round of wood to be split on the block, place it off-center, as far away from you as possible. This gives a little more room for the axe to land on the block in any follow-through after the splitting action.

To start, position yourself in front of the block and square on, with a neutral body position. Hold the axe with a grip from your dominant hand near to the head. Grip near the swell with your nondominant hand. The handle of the axe is across, in front of your body.

Now lift the head of the axe, keeping your grip just below the head and allowing the rest of the handle and your other hand to follow. In a way you can think of this as starting to throw the axe up into the air. Indeed, I often refer to this part of the swing as a throw, as opposed to a lift. This is especially useful when using heavier axes.

As the axe continues to rise both in height and toward the vertical, allow your dominant hand to slide down the handle toward the hand that is already at the swell. Complete this motion with the axe vertical and both of your hands at the base of the handle. If you've used the right amount of energy to throw the axe up, it should feel like the axe comes to a natural halt as your hands come into position. The axe stalls in the air before it begins to fall, in the same way that if you throw a tennis ball up in the air it comes to stop momentarily before falling to the ground again. At this point the axe should feel pretty much weightless.

As the axe begins to fall, this marks the beginning of the downward swing toward the wood that you are about to split. During this downward part of the motion, your hands have two jobs. First and foremost, their job is to guide the axe onto its target. With a heavier axe, or a piece of wood that does not take much splitting, this is potentially all you really need to do. Gravity, the weight of the axe, and the sharpness of its edge will do the rest. You do, however, have the option of applying the second of the two jobs for your hands, which is imparting some extra impetus to the motion of the axe. This additional acceleration, over and above that provided by gravity, comes from your back, not from your arms.

As the axe begins to accelerate downward under the force of gravity, you can add to the acceleration by tensing your lower back and hinging somewhat, transferring this flick into your arms and so the axe. This takes a little practice, but it is ultimately very effective when you need it.

To gain a better picture in your mind, look at the two sequences over the page showing both the throw and the drop, with some extra impetus from the back.

The Throw

1. *The starting position.*

2. *Lifting the axe. Your dominant hand remains near the axe head.*

3. *As the axe is thrown upward, allow your hand to slide down the helve to meet the other.*

4. *As the axe reaches the apex of its motion, both hands meet and take full control.*

5. *The hands control the downward motion.*

The Drop (with acceleration)

1. *The axe approaches the apex on the upward throw.*

2. *As the axe begins to fall, I tense my lower back and push my backside backward. At this point my body position resembles that of a church bell ringer. Then I can effectively pull the axe downward out of the air, generating extra acceleration.*

3. *Impact. Again note the position of the back. The bending of my knees is partially related to the height of the block. See more on this later in chapter 3.*

4. *By starting with the wooden round on the far side of the block to where I am standing, the follow-through of the axe is into the block, not into thin air.*

Small Splitting

Another fundamental use of the axe for producing suitable fuel for fires, at the opposite end of the spectrum to making large movements with larger axes, is splitting down material into small-enough pieces. Small pieces of dry wood split from larger pieces have multiple uses in fire lighting and fire management. In circumstances when you cannot find twigs for kindling or sticks for small firewood in a suitably dry condition for starting a fire, splitting out dry fuel from dead standing wood is a reliable means of obtaining the small-sized fuel you need.

Another situation where I've used the techniques highlighted in this section is on camping spots in popular recreational parks, where kindling is scarce because all the obvious small, dead sticks have been used.

Being able to take dead standing wood of modest size, cut it to length, then split it down provides all the sizes of fuel you need without any fuss or stress.

1. *Split wood has a multitude of uses in camp.*

2. *Kindling, hearth, and feathersticks in Northern Temperate woodland, all produced from split wood.*

3. *Starting a fire in cold conditions in the boreal forest, using split wood.*

I'm putting an emphasis on splitting wood in this way to provide materials for fire lighting and fire management, but the techniques are by no means limited to just this purpose. It is, however, the purpose for which you are most likely going to use them.

The Basics—Working on a Stump

As emphasized in the previous sections regarding axe safety, kneeling is the best way to mitigate risk of injury when using a short-handled axe on a low block or stump.

Most splitting techniques are very dynamic, requiring fast movement of the axe. They also require good aim—hitting the wood in the right place to split it. If you are standing a round of wood on its end, aiming to hit it with an axe, this becomes increasingly difficult the smaller the diameter of the wood. It also becomes harder to balance the wood on the block in the first place.

The technique I'm sharing with you here involves much less dynamic movement of the axe combined with easier aiming. In fact, you do the aiming first, before you swing the axe.

What you are going to do is place the bit of the axe onto the round of wood toward one end. The handle of the axe runs pretty much parallel to the wood you want to split, along the line you want to split it.

1. *Kneeling in front of the low block, hold the wood you want to split over the block. Taking the axe in your dominant hand, place the bit of the axe over the end of the round of wood that is farthest away from you, holding the wood and axe together.*

2. *Side view of body position and how the axe is placed on top of the wood.*

3. *Detail of where the axe bit is placed on the wood, all above the low block.*

4. Detail on hand positioning. Avoid smashing your knuckles between the axe handle and wood. This is easier if the wood is longer than the axe handle.

5. Now lift the axe and wood up, keeping them together, before returning them to the starting place on the block with more speed.

6. The weight of the axe combined with the sharpness of the cutting edge will embed the axe into the wood. You often need to do little more than tap the wood and axe down together to achieve this. With easy-to-split pieces, this will be all you need to split the wood.

Make Life as Easy as Possible—Be Efficient

Knotty wood is harder to split than wood without significant knots. From the perspective of splitting, knots effectively create a peg through the wood, holding it together. This makes a knotty log—even a small, relatively thin one—harder to split. So try to select the least knotty pieces of wood to split. This starts with how you cut the wood down to the lengths you want to split.

1. *Pines and other conifers often have concentrations of knots in one section of their trunk. Start by removing these from one end of the piece you want to split. These can always be burned once the fire is started.*

2. *Being intelligent in how you section up the wood you are going to split will save time and effort later. Making the splitting easier also makes it less likely to result in an injury from the axe.*

3. *A knot-free, small-diameter piece of wood should be the easiest to split.*

Once the piece of wood is split down most of its length, the split can be completed by prizing the axe and wood apart. Right from the start of learning this technique, you should get into the habit of generating the prizing action by moving the wood, not the axe. The reason for this is that the axe will often enter the block after passing through the round of wood you are splitting. Trying to move the axe handle horizontally after it is embedded in a block will result in you trying to rotate the whole block, putting considerable stress on the part of the axe where the head is attached to the handle. Over time this can work to loosen the mating of head and handle.

Once the round has been cleaved in two, exposing the grain inside, splitting tends to become easier from this point onward. Even so, you should work to be as efficient as possible. In particular you should think about the ease of maintaining the axe placement on the wood.

4. *Here the axe bit is embedded in the stump. By twisting the wood horizontally relative to the axe, the split can be opened and the splitting of the wood completed without putting undue stress on the axe.*

5. *Moving the wood, not the axe, to open the split.*

6. *It's easier to balance the axe bit on the flat side of the wood than on the curved side.*

7. *Same technique as before—place the axe on the wood, then raise the two together, returning them to the block with sufficient force to split the wood.*

8. *Again, remember to turn the wood to open the split, leaving the axe static.*

9. *When we get down to quarters, it's easier to place the axe on the curved surface than on the apex opposite it.*

10. *On smaller pieces still, it can be tricky to get the split to run the full length without running off to the side. At this stage, turn the piece on its side and split from there.*

11. *You can split down to really quite small splints with well-selected material and good, efficient technique.*

12. *Examples of the fuel sizes needed for establishing a campfire.*

Dealing with Difficulties

Every piece of wood is unique. Some pieces harbor unseen knots. Some species of tree split more easily than others. Employing this splitting technique won't always be like putting a hot knife through butter.

First off, you should know how to remove the axe from the round of wood, should the wood not split. The critical point is to keep your fingers well out of the way. Levering an axe against a piece of wood creates an excellent guillotine for your fingers. Make sure they are nowhere near the axe head. A second concern, but also important, is what the axe will do when it is free of the wood, as in the "Where Does It Go Next?" section earlier (see page 63). The more force you are applying, the more it can accelerate as soon as there is nothing to oppose the force. Make sure the axe is not going to come out toward your arm or drop onto your leg once it is free.

1. *When levering an axe from a round of wood, make sure your hands are nowhere near the bit of the axe. Also make sure the axe is not going to spring free toward you, particularly onto one of your arms or legs.*

2. *With the split started, you can attempt to continue the split by placing the axe farther back and opening it up farther, using the same technique as before. Note, however, how the wood has been moved forward so the axe bit remains over the block.*

3. *Once split, it's back to the same basic technique.*

4. *Gnarly bits of wood don't always split cleanly. Don't stress, though, since this wood is not going to make good feathersticks anyway!*

5. *Knots cause the most problems for this technique. You might have split the log in half with no problem, but then a knot like this can cause one of the resulting halves to be difficult to split.*

6. *Here you can see the knot going right through to the other side of the piece.*

7. *The answer to knots is usually to attack them directly with the axe and split them too if possible.*

8. *Success. To finish the split, again the piece is turned while keeping the axe static.*

The above splitting technique is one of the most useful I know. For producing suitable fuel sizes for campfires or wood stoves, this technique is particularly valuable. It's certainly the most frequently used around camp, whether close to home or on wilderness journeys. I've used it from canoe trips in Canada in the summer to winter camping trips in the far northern parts of Scandinavia.

While the emphasis here has been on taking rounds of wood that you can hold in your hand to split down, you can equally apply it to pieces of wood of a similar size that have been split down from larger rounds still. Indeed, this makes sense in combination with splitting larger rounds on a chopping block. The time to switch to the hand-splitting technique is the point at which the split pieces become difficult to balance on the chopping block, and harder to aim for even if they do remain balanced.

Moreover, due to it being less dynamic and more controlled than many freehand splitting techniques, it is relatively safe to use in confined spaces and near other people.

Optimal Use of a Chopping Block

Splitting on a Low Block

Unless you are in your backyard, often the block you'll have use of will be low. It may not have been cut as a chopping block at all. Remember the context. We are looking at techniques for the woods and for use while on the trail. In your yard, it would be worth the investment in time and effort to obtain a chopping block that suits you best, at a height that is most comfortable for you. In contrast, the random piece of discarded, sawn wood you'll end up using out on a trip will not be your perfect chopping block from home. Even in a temporary or semipermanent camp being used as a base, you may well not have anything other than a low block. So, it's worth knowing how to make the best use of low blocks, both in terms of efficiency and safety.

Splitting on a Low Block with a Small Axe

In keeping with the general safety principles covered at the beginning of this chapter, for a low block you make the situation much safer if you kneel to use a short axe. In the context of a block, you are going to be working on the far side of the block rather than the closest part. So for splitting, place each piece to be split on the far side of the block, away from you. This means that if you strike too close or glance off the wood in front of you, the next thing the axe hits is the block. A common occurrence, though, is for someone to strike too far away. There is a tendency, when kneeling, to kneel too close. When you swing an axe with any weight, your arms tend to extend and straighten at the elbow. When inexperienced people first size up with an axe, they tend to underestimate how far away the axe bit will strike. The result is the axe handle hitting the piece of wood, rather than the axe head. This leads to overstrike damage to the axe handle.

1. *Placing the log to be split on the far side of the block means any glancing blows or shortfalls still hit the block.*

2. *Somewhat exaggerated here, but not uncommon, is the tendency to bend the arms at the elbow when sizing up the cut.*

3. *When the axe is swung with force, the arms become more extended. You end up with the handle hitting the wood and the potential for overstrike damage.*

4. *Kneel farther away and stretch the arms out to represent a realistic splitting strike.*

5. *Then you hit your target.*

Splitting on a Low Block with a Large Axe

When using a heavier axe with a longer handle to split on a low block, kneeling is not necessary. Plus, a more powerful swing can be made standing up. Due to the weight of the axe, we can use gravity to help us do the splitting work.

As with the smaller axe, you should size things up when you first pick up the axe, making sure you are at an appropriate distance from the block. Don't forget to place the piece on the farthest extent of the block. With the larger axe swinging down toward your feet, that backstop of block is important.

You can also improve the safety and efficiency of the swing by bending your knees to bring the axe handle more horizontal at the point the axe head hits the piece you are splitting. This modifies the path of the axe head from an arc toward you as you pivot from the shoulder joints to a more vertical drop toward the block as you bend your knees.

The adjustment made by bending the knees means the cutting edge of the axe is hitting the wood straight down, which is a more efficient cut. It's also safer, especially on a low block.

The key then is to follow through as much as necessary, again taking full advantage of gravity pulling the axe head downward. Modifying the swing by bending your knees puts the axe on a more vertical path, rather than standing straight, with the resultant arc of the axe bringing it toward you and the ground as you rotate the swing from your shoulder.

1. *Standing up straight results in the full-size axe striking the top of the log at an angle, toe first.*

2. *Bending at the knees results in the axe bit striking the top of the log vertically.*

3. *This sequence shows a strong strike with the full-size axe. Bending at the knees modifies the path of the axe from an arc toward me to a safer and more effective vertical path through the log to the chopping block. (Photos in this sequence by John Cummings)*

3a

3c

3b

3d

Splitting Firewood When You Have No Block

When on a wilderness journey, such as a summer canoe trip or winter snow walk, unless you are camping at a spot where you or someone else has previously left or created a chopping block, you will not have one to work on. Yet, if you are using fire for boiling water, cooking, or warmth, you may well have to split wood.

It's never a good idea to split directly onto soil, since it contains small stones and smaller particles of grit.

Solid rock in camping spots, such as in the Canadian Shield country, is even more potentially damaging to axe bits. Snow presents almost an opposite problem, in that you have no solid surface onto which you can work. After creating a trampled snow platform, even one that has formed a decent crust overnight, if you place a round of wood on top of it and start imparting downward blows with the axe, the wood will quickly punch through the platform.

Continuous solid rock and little topsoil is characteristic of the Canadian Shield. Note the various sizes of split wood on the right, prepared using the techniques in this section.

Dead, standing pine cut into lengths for the tent stove.

Switching to the Horizontal

If you can't work vertically because the surface upon which you are operating is too hard or too soft, then working horizontally can provide the solution. You'll need a couple of extra techniques. You should bear in mind, right from the outset, that these techniques are dynamic; indeed, they work only if the axe is moving at speed. Your safety, as well as the safety of others around you, requires you to strictly adhere to the safety points included here.

Between the Legs

This is a technique for the half axe. Longer axes are too long and hatchets are too short. The idea is that the round of wood you want to split is placed on the snow, rock, or ground close to horizontal; then the front surface of the round is struck with the axe, sharply and with speed. While the idea is simple, there are a couple of important details. The front surface (the surface you will strike with the axe) should be raised very slightly by using a small piece of wood. This has a couple of benefits. First, it raises your target off the ground, which means you are less likely to clip ground or rock with the toe of the axe bit. Second, the lower edge of the rear surface of the log gains some purchase on the snow, rock, or ground, reducing its ability to move easily. On snow, this slight angle to the horizontal can also be achieved by placing the rear face of the round of wood into a depression in the snow.

Between-the-legs splitting technique being used on a snow platform.

Key safety points:

1. Find a safe area, away from where other people in your camp are operating. Make sure your companions are aware of what you are doing, and tell them to stay away from you, especially to avoid moving around in the vicinity directly in front or behind you. Once you have your head down to swing the axe, it's unlikely you will see anyone approaching. Tell people not to try to collect the firewood you are splitting until you have stopped swinging the axe and said it is OK to approach.

2. Once a round is placed on the ground in the position you are going to strike it with the axe, it is imperative you position your feet such that your heels are no farther back than the front surface of the round of wood. This ensures that the axe is already past your legs if you miss the wood, or if the axe deflects from, or through, the wood at an unexpected angle. That is, ensure that the follow-through is not your foot, ankle, or shin.

3. Think about what you want to hit, not what you want to avoid. You want to hit the wood, not your feet. As you ride a bicycle down an otherwise flat street, if you focus on the one pothole you'll tend toward it, rather than away from it. Focus on where you want to go, not what you want to avoid. Likewise here, with the axe, think about what you want to hit.

4. Do not let go of the axe. This may seem obvious, but it happens. Contrary to what many think, letting go of the axe will not send it flying a long distance behind you. Rather, your grip tends to weaken toward the end of the stroke, when the axe is on an upward arc. If you let go of the axe, it will tend to go upward and be spinning above you or closely behind. You should be mindful of the reduction in sensitivity and dexterity that even thin leather gloves can bring. Don't attempt this technique with gloves that don't provide a good grip on the axe handle; for example, wool or synthetic-material gloves with no grippy palm.

5. Do not partially let go of the axe. In a way, partially letting go of the axe is actually worse than fully letting go. While you might injure yourself if you let go, you will definitely injure yourself if you partially let go in the way I describe below. I have never done this, but I have seen a photograph of an example of the result. The individual, keeping only a few fingers in contact with the grip of the axe handle, ended up with a deep cut to their lower back, just to the side of their spine, as the axe was able to swing upward, with their fingers as the pivot point.

6. Remove any lanyard that may be attached to the axe. A lanyard attaching the axe to your arm is a liability. You absolutely do not want a sharp, three-dimensional pendulum attached to the end of your arm, flailing unpredictably between your legs.

So, given these safety concerns, why bother with this technique at all? Well, necessity. As described, there are some situations where you have no block. Plus, it's a beautifully efficient technique when used in the right circumstances and executed correctly.

Your grip should be two-handed. As to which hand is top and which is bottom, this is a matter of personal choice. Most people initially opt for their nondominant hand to be nearest the swell of the handle (the guide hand), and their dominant hand above it, which is how you naturally hold an axe with two hands. But for this technique, some people prefer the opposite arrangement, with their dominant hand guiding. Either way, go through the motions gently at first and see which feels most comfortably in control for you. That's the one to choose.

Wood-processing area on a winter hot-tenting trip.

1. *A student getting to grips with the between-the-legs technique. A two-handed grip ensures the axe remains on the body's centerline.*

2. *The axe is swung swiftly, aiming for a sharp yet accurate impact on the face of the wood being split.*

3. *The wood is split almost along its entire length but has also moved off a little distance because it is a little light.*

Get a free video demonstrating the dynamics of the between-the-legs technique at
wildernessaxekills.com/resources

The Side Swing

This is a technique for axes longer than the half axe; ones that you can't swing between your legs due to the length of the handle being such that the head would hit the ground. Like the between-the-legs technique, this swing needs to be swift. I particularly like this technique with a three-quarter axe, since the relative lack of weight compared to a full-size axe means the axe accelerates quickly. Moreover, for me it's of particular relevance to the three-quarter axe, since this is my preferred size of axe for boreal forest trips in winter.

Like the hand of a clock on the wall, as the axe moves farther away from the six o'clock position of the between-the-legs technique, it gets higher off the ground. Hence, you can obtain the ground clearance you need for longer axes by swinging the axe to the side of your legs, rather than in between. The question then becomes this: Which side? Most people will naturally hold their nondominant hand closest to the swell and their dominant hand above this, nearer the head. This means that swinging the axe to the side of the nondominant hand is the way to go. As with other two-handed techniques, though, some find it more natural to swing the axe to the other side, with their hands switched. Either way, swing the axe to the side of the hand that is closest to the end of the handle.

Place the round of wood on the ground, snow, or rock. Raise the front edge as before. You will then need to size up how far away from the log to stand, so the axe is the correct distance off the ground to hit the wood where you want to strike it and start the split. Make sure your heels are no farther back than the front face of the log. Once you have measured up and are in position, raise the axe and swing swiftly and crisply.

Key safety points: The safety points largely echo the safety points of the between-the-legs technique. In particular, ensure you have a safe area, and your companions are aware to stay clear. If you accidentally let go of the axe during this technique, it will tend to go farther away from you than it would in the between-the-legs technique, so make sure the area behind you is clear. From my perspective, it's easier to keep hold of the axe here because your legs don't impede your arms toward the end of the swing like they can with the earlier technique. Here your arms can follow through with the axe. Don't turn this into a golf swing, though. You don't want to be swinging your axe around behind your head and back. Before you swing, remember to position yourself ahead of the front face of the log, so that it is physically impossible for any follow-through of the axe swing to be toward your legs.

1. *In the correct position for the side swing. (Photo by Craig Taylor)*

2. *A swift strike with the three-quarter axe and the log is split. (Photo by Craig Taylor)*

1

2

Some Pointers

Here are some tips to help you with these dynamic techniques.

As with much of bushcraft, material selection is important. These techniques work better on wood that is relatively straight grained and reasonably low in knots. If there are predictable knots in the wood you are processing, such as the regularly spaced rings of knots you get with pines, then saw the wood so the ring of knots is at one end of the round of wood, rather than in the middle. Then initially attack the round from the opposite end to where the knots are.

These techniques depend on the inertia of the wood. This is why the axe needs to move swiftly. The axe penetrates the round, with the split being initiated before the wood has had a chance to accelerate away from the blow. These techniques work better on heavier bits of wood. If the wood is light, it will accelerate quickly.

The longer the piece of wood, the more difficult it becomes to get the split to run all the way along the piece. If you want a general rubric, then I would suggest that once you reach lengths of wood beyond 2 ft. (60 cm), you are making your life more difficult than if you saw the wood shorter and undertake more splitting.

These techniques become harder the smaller the target area at the end of the round of wood. This is partly related to the inertia point above, since there is less mass in the log. It's also about the accuracy you need to hit the end of the log. You can build up a high degree of accuracy with an axe for these techniques. And with some species of wood, you can almost merely flick the axe and the wood will split. Equally, though, time and energy are important resources, particularly while making a wilderness journey. If you can pick the round up in one hand, then I would move to the hand-splitting technique described elsewhere (see pages 71–77).

Aim to hit the piece of wood in the upper half, rather than across the middle. You want the split to move down through the piece as well as back through it. Better to start the split on the outside than in the middle. With smaller pieces of wood this may mean clipping the wood with part of the axe's cutting edge, rather than its full extent.

If the wood does not split the first time, remove the axe if necessary, reset the piece of wood in position, then try again, hitting in line with the axe mark you already made. If the piece splits only part of the way—not all the way through—turn the wood around and attack it from the other end, aiming to hit the face in line with the partial split at the other end, with the intention of the two meeting.

The Opportunistic Tree Stump

Oftentimes you have to haul dead standing wood away from where you felled it to where you are camping. Sometimes, though, the two places are close by, in which case there are some advantages to limbing, sectioning, and splitting the wood right where you felled it. One of the advantages is that you can use the tree stump of the tree you felled as the chopping block, even though it will not be much larger in diameter than what you are splitting and will be quite low down. You will have to saw off the top of the stump to remove the remnants of your felling cuts, leaving the surface flat and horizontal. You can then not only more easily process the rounds of wood from the tree you felled close to your camp but also process any further firewood you carry into your camp area.

The small chopping block here is the stump of a tree we felled near our camp.

3. When the axe goes all the way through the round you are splitting, it hits the log underneath, not the ground.

4. If you need to encourage the split along the piece of wood, make sure you reposition the wood so the axe bit remains above the log you are working down onto.

5. Even cutting across the grain of the supporting log, the axe can become embedded.

6. As always, keep the axe stationary, rotating only the piece of wood to leverage the split.

Using a stump for splitting kindling.

Small Firewood and Kindling—Hand-Splitting with No Block

Unlike other splitting techniques, which depend on a log being balanced on a flat surface, this technique, which I introduced earlier in this chapter, does not require a flat surface. You can work onto another log, even a relatively small one.

A note of caution here, though: you should make sure that once the piece of wood has been split, your axe does not continue onward toward the ground. On rock, the potential damaging results should be obvious. Even soft earth containing stones and sandy particles will dull or damage the cutting edge. So, to protect your axe's edge, it's an important consideration to make sure the axe bit is over the log onto which you are splitting. Further, maintaining alignment of the axe bit, the wood you are splitting, and the log you are working onto provides the most effective transmission of force.

1. *Applying the same technique as before, but now onto a small-diameter log*

2. *Make sure the axe bit, wood, and log are all in alignment.*

A student taking onboard the lesson of utilizing what they can find to split onto, rather than directly onto stony ground. (Photo by Ray Goodwin)

Above: Winter camping in northern Sweden. Note the split firewood in the foreground, including the horizontal logs for splitting onto, using the techniques in this section.

Below: Splints and other sizes of fuel stacked neatly alongside the stove during a winter camping trip in a heated tent.

Splitting Larger Logs with Smaller Axes

When we are journeying it is highly unlikely we will have access to a splitting axe unless we are staying in a cabin where there is one already. Much more likely on a trip is that we have one general-purpose axe with us. Moreover, this is most likely to be a half axe or a three-quarter axe. We may, however, still want to or even need to split quite large rounds for firewood. Another scenario that might provide some splitting difficulties is one where the firewood, while not particularly large, could be quite knotty and difficult to split with a general-purpose axe profile.

So it's useful for us to have some extra tricks up our sleeve for use with our general-purpose axe. We can of course baton the axe. Elsewhere in this book I even show you how to make a hefty mallet (see page 124), which would be very good for this job. We can also use wooden wedges (also known as gluts) to help split intransigent rounds of wood. We would of course have to make these, but it can be worthwhile if we have a large amount of difficult bits of wood to split. This is shown in a later chapter (see page 122), as is how to use them to split a longer piece lengthwise (see page 120).

But what if during our general firewood-splitting session we encounter the occasional log that is a bit too much for our small axe? Well, we can use what I like to call the upside-down technique. Remember that our small axes are relatively light. This is one of the reasons why we carry them in preference over larger, heavier axes on journeys where weight is important. With limited head weight and a narrow cross section compared to splitting axes, there is a limit to what we can expect of our travel axes though.

The Upside-Down Technique

There is a useful shift in thinking following the realization that the log we are trying to split may weigh considerably more than the axe we are using to split it. Gravity is our friend here. Rather than trying to drive a really quite lightweight axe downward into a heavy log, it makes more sense to drive the heavy log downward onto the axe. Now, I'm not proposing you somehow fix your axe to the ground or the chopping block and throw logs at it. Once you have given your best shot to split the log with your axe, particularly if the axe is firmly embedded in the log, it's a relatively simple job to invert the situation and then drop the axe down again with the log on top.

Larger rounds of wood can be split with small axes in combination with a mallet and wooden wedges.

There are two things you need to protect here. The first is your back. The second is your axe. Potential damage to either arises from leverage. We've already established that the log we are dealing with is quite heavy, so lifting it up requires us to be smart so that we protect our assets, as well as being energy efficient.

The lift, as I call it, is an extension of how to lift an axe head efficiently anyway. Rather than trying to lift the axe and the block of wood from the end of the handle, you slide your hand forward so that it is as close to the head as possible. This puts much less stress on your wrist and forearms, and, in comparison, lifting the whole package of axe and log feels easy from this point. This method of lifting from the head prolongs the life of the axe by putting far less stress on the interface between the head and the handle.

Once you have your hand in position to lift near the axe head, you then want to move your body closer to the objects you are lifting. This puts less strain on your shoulder and less leverage on your back. You are basically stepping underneath the axe and log as you lift it up, all in one smooth motion.

One safety point here, though, is that you don't want to get your face over the axe head as you lift, because if it separates from the log, you are suddenly lifting something much lighter with an excessive amount of force. You do not want to hit yourself in the face with the axe poll.

Upside-Down Technique: The Lift
In the sequence below, I show the lift. (Photos by Amanda Quaine)

1. *Having swung my three-quarter axe at this log, it has become embedded, but the log has not split.*

2. *I step in, sliding my hand toward the head.*

3. *I slide my hand as far forward as possible.*

4. *Taking a firm grip of the axe, I bend my knee and my arm and take the strain.*

5. *Stepping in with my left foot, I now begin to draw the axe and the head up and away from the stump, toward my body.*

4

7

5

8

6

6. *Drawing my elbow in toward my ribs, I lock my arm into a relatively strong position, taking the weight of the axe and the log.*

7. *Rotating my body, I bring the axe and the log to a position where I can smoothly move it up onto my shoulder.*

8. *Using the momentum I generated in the first part of the motion, I bring the log and the axe up to my shoulder while moving my elbow underneath, so that my arm is locked into a vertical position. As I do so, I'm also pulling down somewhat on the end of the handle, which provides a degree of leverage and control.*

9. *Straightening my legs and my back in addition to raising my right arm a little more while dropping my left, I complete the lift to a point where I can begin to drop the axe, poll first, onto the chopping block, with the round of wood above it.*

10. *Finally, as I begin to tip the axe and log forward, I bend at the waist and the knee, ready for the drop.*

Upside-Down Technique: The Drop

The author demonstrating this technique with a half axe at a bushcraft event in the UK. (Photos by Martin Tomlinson)

1. *As the log and axe are projected forward from my shoulder, I slide my hand back from the head. I'm bending my legs a fair bit here, since I'm working on a low block. The aim is to have the axe land poll down, handle horizontal, with the log stacked vertically on top of the axe's cutting edge.*

2. *The moment of impact. The axe stops dead as it hits the block, while the momentum of the log causes it to split itself on the stationary axe.*

3. *The two halves of the split log are ejected by the force of impact. Note the axe handle is horizontal.*

A few final points about this technique: the first is one of safety. There is potential for logs to go flying off the chopping block toward bystanders. As with any chopping on a block, make sure you have enough room around you. Second, and related to the first: the less vertically the axe and log hit the stump, the less force is imparted directly down onto the cutting edge of the axe, with more of the movement being converted into the log rotating off the top of the axe head. At the point at which the axe hits the block, the whole unit of axe and log should be traveling vertically. This also means that the log or logs are less likely to go tumbling off the block any great distance.

You may be asking, what if I have no block? Good question, but remember, to be undertaking the upside-down technique, you most likely have some sizeable rounds of wood to split. So use one of the bigger rounds as your block. If you have only one round, keep it as the block to split smaller pieces onto.

1

3

2

Small-Scale Felling and Clearing

Here we are going to consider taking down small trees. By small I mean trees of a weight that you could pick up after felling. These are trees that are really just growing up from being saplings. There isn't a lot of weight to them, so there isn't a huge amount of consideration required in terms of the felling cuts and safety precautions around the felling of larger and weighty trees. We cover this serious business in the next chapter (see page 100).

This doesn't mean we should just start hacking at small trees without any form of consideration or diligence though. When it comes to taking down smaller trees, we have a couple of options in terms of the tools that we use. We can use a bow saw for the whole job, or we can use an axe. Some jobs may be much easier with a small pruning saw. Many small felling jobs can be done quickly and easily with an axe, provided you have access to the stem or the trunk of what you want to take out. For example, all a wrist-thickness birch needs is a quick couple of cuts in from the right, then switch to holding the axe the other way around (more on ambidextrous axe use in chapter 4, page 117), followed by a couple more cuts from the left into the base of the same V-shaped cut. The aim is to be efficient.

Clear access is not always available, though, simply because you may have multiple small trees growing close together, as is often the case with birches, or multiple shoots all growing up from the same root system, which is often the case with hazel or willow. The other consideration that we have is whether or not the materials we are taking are part of an ongoing coppicing-rotation system, sometimes encountered in European forests.

Even if the tree has not been coppiced, ask yourself if the species would benefit from being left tidy enough for it to regrow. Some widespread species, such as hazels, willows, and even some birches, can regrow multiple shoots from a stump if the stump is left in good condition.

Left: *Many trunks and shoots growing from the same European hazel root system.*

A traditionally coppiced species that occurs near to where I teach courses is sweet chestnut, *Castanea sativa*. This species will grow into a large tree of a similar stature to an oak if left unmolested but once cut, it will grow multiple shoots off the same root bole.

The trunk of a large sweet chestnut tree that has never been coppiced.

Many trunks growing from the same sweet chestnut specimen that has been coppiced multiple times.

So, consideration of which tool to use is not only about the ease and efficacy for us personally. It's also a question of how we want to leave the remainder of what we don't take. So, even if it may be quicker to make a couple of cuts with an axe, it might be more appropriate to saw carefully with a pruning saw.

Then, once you have the material you've felled, there is a question of how to remove unwanted side branches from the trunk you've harvested. Sometimes it's easy just to take off a few small twigs and branches with your belt knife. Sometimes it can be easier to resort to a pruning saw. Sometimes even small trees are densely foliated, and here I'm thinking in particular of birch saplings and spruces. In these situations it can be much quicker and easier to lop off all the little branches by using a half or three-quarter axe.

The author cleaning branches from small spruce trees with a half axe. (Photo by Stuart Wittke)

A primary rule is that you want to approach this process of removing the branches from one end of the tree, then work methodically toward the other. You may be wondering from which end should you start. There is a right end and a wrong end. To determine which is which, you need to look at how the branches are growing. Many deciduous trees grow with their branches angled upward of the horizontal, creating a smaller angle between the top of the branch and the vertical trunk than the larger angle between the bottom of the branch and vertical. That is, the branches are reaching upward. By contrast, many needled species, such as spruces, grow with their branches angled downward to the horizontal, which means there is a larger angle between the vertical and the top of the branch and a smaller angle between the vertical and the bottom of the branch.

The general principle for clearing the branches, then, is to trim the branches from the side of the larger angle. With needled species this will often be from the top to the bottom, and with deciduous species this will often be from the bottom to the top. But the general rule is to go with cutting from the more open angle.

The birch tree in the foreground has branches and twigs angled upward.
This is typical of many deciduous tree species.

Spruces and many other species of needled tree typically have their
branches angled downward.

Felling, Limbing, and Sectioning

Assessing Trees for Felling

I'll start this chapter by stressing several very important points. First, felling trees is dangerous. Second, you are (probably) not a trained arborist, and, third, keep life simple when it comes to felling.

It's sometimes necessary to take down a tree (or the remaining part of a tree) that is making a camping spot unsafe. Otherwise you have a choice of what you fell. Moreover, you are under no obligation to fell anything. My advice is to keep the felling you undertake as straightforward as possible. Half-fallen trees are difficult to deal with, especially with limited equipment. When a tree first starts to fall, it has very little speed or momentum. It is easy for a relatively small branch touching from a nearby tree to stall the fall in its early stages. If you are choosing to take down a dead tree for firewood or a live tree for materials, make sure it is clear of other trees that could interfere with its fall. Also, make sure the tree will fall into a clear area. If you are not well practiced at dropping trees, then think twice about trying to achieve pinpoint accuracy with where the tree has to fall for it to come down cleanly.

Then look at the lean of the tree. Is the tree leaning the way you want it to go? Or is it leaning in the opposite direction, or off to the side? Don't just look up at the tree from a distance. Stand at the base of the tree and look up. Once you have a general idea of which direction the tree will want to fall, you can obtain an even better idea of precisely where the tree is going to fall by standing with your back to the tree trunk, then looking up. A further factor to assess is whether there are more branches on one side of the tree than any other. This may help or hinder the tree in falling in the direction you want it to. A final factor that can help or hinder the tree's fall is wind. If strong enough, wind can push a tree in the opposite direction to which it would otherwise go. Wind also moves trees around a fair amount and may increase the risk of the trunk splitting as you start to fell the tree.

1. *Get under the trees and look up.*

2. *Look up to see which way the trees are leaning, as well as which side has the most branches.*

3. *Making an assessment of which way the tree wants to fall.*

An axe and a saw allow you to access larger timber for your projects.

Felling Trees with Axe and Saw

Proficient felling of a well-chosen tree can seem effortlessly straightforward. On the other hand, ill-thought-out felling can become complicated and dangerous. Either way, felling is one of the more hazardous endeavors in the woods. In this section I want to highlight the main points I teach to people when learning to fell trees. I will assume you have basic axe-handling skills and good general axe safety awareness.

Why Might You Need to Fell Sizeable Trees?

There are a number of good reasons why you may need to fell sizeable trees. The need for firewood is a common one, particularly in winter conditions. Dead, standing timber is the best source of dry firewood in the forest. If you are building a long-log fire, then you need logs of a good diameter. Even if you are using smaller fuel, it may be most efficient to source it from a dead, standing tree than split it down. A second reason you may need to take down a tree is to make a camping spot safe. I've had to do this a few times on canoe trips, where the campsite has been compromised by an unsafe tree. You might think, Why didn't you just move? Well, these situations arose either on islands in rivers or in areas of thick bush where there was an established, albeit small, camping spot. Third, you may need materials for woodcraft projects. This could be the wood itself, the bark, or both.

Tools for the Job

Your primary tool for felling is an axe. You can use a half axe and upward for felling. Hatchets are too small and light. You can fell entirely with an axe, but it is somewhat more controlled if you use a saw in combination with your axe to complete the felling. On trips I tend to carry a folding bucksaw that breaks down and folds into a relatively compact shape.

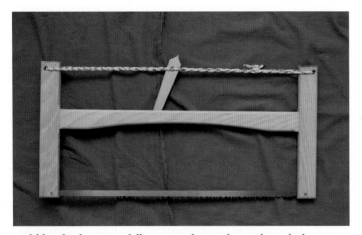

A folding bucksaw is a full-size saw that is also easily packed.

A half axe and an improvised bow saw.

Left: In the boreal forest in winter, fire is your friend. This type of long-log fire is a traditional Scandinavian survival fire that needs big logs.

Principles of Felling

First, it's worth us stepping back for a moment to think about the structure of a tree trunk. It is a bundle of fibers fixed to the ground at one end. Like any upright structure, the weight bears down through the structure. And like a stick, if you bend it, you put the fibers on the outside of the curve under tension, and those on the inside of the curve under compression.

Use this understanding of the structure of the trunk to help your felling. First remove some of the wood from the trunk on the side you want the tree to fall toward. This action removes the support the tree has on one side and should create a small lean in the tree. This puts the outside fibers on the opposite side of the trunk under tension. You can then cut these fibers—almost one by one—until the tree begins to fall.

First make the front cut—sometimes called the gob cut—with the axe. This is a wedge-shaped cut, the center of which should be the direction you want the tree to fall. Cut back into the tree no farther than halfway through the trunk. The base of the cut is horizontal and the top of the cut is angled, such that as the tree falls, the top will not touch the bottom until the tree trunk is at least half the way toward the ground. The back of this cut, where the two angles come together, is at right angles to the direction of fall.

Once you have completed the front cut, you need to make a cut at the back. It is possible to make back cuts with an axe, but it is less controlled than with a saw. A saw is a great tool for the job, actually. Because the fibers at the back should now be under tension, there is little chance the saw blade is pinched. You can cut in gradually with the saw in a very controlled manner.

1. *Inspecting a front cut.*

2. *Highlighting the line on which the tree will fall, using the handle of my axe.*

At this stage I should say that you must not pass in front of the tree once you have begun the back cut. You are in the process of destabilizing the tree. Nor should you walk too close to the back of the tree behind the direction the tree wants to fall. Therefore you should have both your axe and saw with you before you begin.

The base of your front cut should be horizontal. Your back cut is also going to be horizontal. To achieve this, you cut horizontally with your saw. Ensure that the blade is running parallel to the back of the front cut, so you are cutting symmetrically behind the front cut. The critical point—sometimes displayed incorrectly in books—is that the back cut must be made above the bottom face of the front cut. About 1 in. (2.5 cm) is a good distance to start above the line of the bottom of the front cut. This gives some margin for error if the saw dips down while cutting.

Why is the relationship between the position of the front cut and back cut so important? Well, it creates two mechanical features that make the fall of the tree more controlled and predictable. Putting the back cut above the bottom of the front cut creates a step. The back of this step forms a backstop for the base of the tree as it falls. This stops the trunk from slipping backward off the stump and provides a stable pivot point.

During the process of making your back cut, the tree will begin to fall. Usually the saw blade won't reach the front cut before the tree starts to fall. Once you have cut enough fibers at the back of the tree, it will be free to move away. So you will usually end up with an area in between the front cut and the back cut where the fibers remain attached. These connected fibers we call a hinge. Only when the trunk pulls away from the stump will these fibers disconnect.

3. *Start cutting the back cut as horizontal as possible.*

4. *Keep the blade of the saw parallel to the back line of the front cut.*

5. *The step created by making the back cut (right of photo) higher than the lower face of the front cut. (left of photo)*

6. *Tree caught midfall in this photo. You can see the back cut opening up and the base of the trunk pivoting against the back of the step.*

7. The author pointing out the area between the front cut and back cut that formed the hinge.

8. The long fibers in the center of the stump remain after being pulled out of the base of the trunk as it fell off the stump.

9. Looking at the base of a tree trunk after felling. The upper face of the front cut (left), the torn hinge fibers (center), and the back cut (right) are evident.

10. Stumps of dead, standing pine trees felled for firewood at a winter camp.

The accompanying images of felled live and dead trees all show good examples of hinges. Something can go wrong, though. Rather than pivoting from the step, with a nice hinge in place, the tree can split up the middle of the trunk, then pivot from a point higher up. The trunk still comes down to the ground, but the section of trunk from the back cut up the pivot will be levered up and away from the tree at the back of the trunk. This is a major reason why you or your companions should never stand or kneel behind the tree. Work from the side of the tree. This pivoting from higher up, with a section of the trunk being turned skyward, is called a barber's chair. If the lower end catches you it could be extremely injurious, if not lethal.

Before You Start

First, after selecting your tree and assessing direction of fall, you should ensure that you have a clear workspace at the base of the tree. You don't want to be tripping or rolling your ankle while using your axe or moving in the vicinity. Nor do you want the use of your axe or saw to be impeded by nearby vegetation or shoots from the base of the tree. Check that there is nothing nearby that might catch your axe as you swing it.

Once you have your work area cleared, determine your escape routes. You must be able to move away from the tree as it starts to fall. For obvious reasons, you do not want to move in the same direction as the falling tree. For reasons explained above, moving directly behind the tree can also be hazardous. So back and away at around 45 degrees is the general rule. Satisfy yourself that you can move swiftly along your route without tripping or slipping. Remove anything that may impede your safe retreat.

Finally, if you have companions with you, be clear with them that you are felling trees. Make sure you know where they are, and, if they're in the vicinity of where you are felling (e.g., watching), make sure they are at a safe distance away, off to the side or a safe distance behind where the tree will fall.

Even dead, dry trees are heavy. Live trees increase the weight involved multiple times. The weights coming down to the ground, even in a modest tree, are surprising. The leverage a tall trunk can apply at its base is colossal. Always take great care to apply the safety considerations listed.

Left: *Determine your escape route before starting to fell.*

Efficient Limbing of Felled Trees

Regardless of whether the tree is alive or dead, or what the end use of the tree is, there are typically two main processing jobs you will need to complete. First, you will need to remove the tree's limbs; that is, its branches. This is known as limbing or snedding. Second, you will need to cut the tree into sections, a task described as sectioning or bucking.

Safety First

In chapter 3 I took a methodical look at fundamental axe safety for day-to-day usage around camp. There I related a series of questions to ask, and here, in the context of limbing and sectioning, they are worth repeating, since they apply 100 percent to these jobs too.

Where does it go next is a question you should always ask when using a cutting tool. What happens if I slip? What happens if it glances off? What happens if it cuts straight through what I'm working on? What happens if I miss? What happens if it bounces off? In each of these cases, where does it go next?

You never want the answer to the question of where it goes next to be part of your body. Especially when it comes to using an axe.

In the context of a felled tree, however, the axe is not the only risk. The tree itself can also pose a threat to your safety. Branches of the tree can be bent and under tension—tension that will release when you start cutting them. Equally, smaller trees may be bent out of position by the felled tree, potentially releasing to their upright position when you start dismantling the felled tree. Be aware of what, if anything, has been spring-loaded by felling the tree before you start work.

If the tree is supported at one or more points along its length, rather than in complete contact with the ground, then, as you cut it, some of the tree could rise up as you change the balance, or part of the trunk could drop to the ground, or both at the same time. Basically, as you cut the trunk you may end up with one or two seesaws that want to move. Be aware of how the tree is resting before you start work. If you are working on sloping ground, pay particular attention to whether or not any section of trunk is likely to drop to the ground when detached from the remainder of the tree, and whether it is likely to roll toward you or your companions.

In a nutshell, think about what the separated bits of the tree you are about to create will do—under the forces of gravity and spring-loading—when you free them from the rest of the tree. There are some other technique-specific safety points in the following relevant sections too.

1. *The indicated strike point on the trunk is just past my knee, and at that point the axe will be moving away from me.*

2. *Technique 1—double-handed grip: I stand square on with my shoulders pretty much parallel to the trunk.*

3. *Technique 2—one-handed grip: I can stand sideways on and effectively cut just behind me, again away from my body.*

4. *The same side-and-behind one-handed technique as above, but with a longer-handled axe. Note I am holding the handle halfway along for more control.*

5. *The axe follows through beyond my body and away from it.*

6. *Working safely past my body even on a small tree.*

Bottom Up

When limbing or snedding a tree, start from one end of the tree and work toward the other. This is partly about being methodical, but also partly about being efficient. It's generally easier to cut off branches, large or small, if you attack them from the less acute angle with the trunk. For example, many needled trees have downward-sloping branches, whereas many broadleaved trees have upward-reaching branches. Attack the branches from the direction they are growing away from. Even if you are removing what are little more than twigs, you'll find it much easier working this way.

Working methodically from the bottom of the tree toward the top.

Techniques

When limbing, you should work as much as possible with the axe on the other side of the trunk to where you are standing. This helps with safety, since it significantly reduces the chance of a glancing blow deflecting toward you. Other times you may have to work on top of the trunk to cut off more vertically oriented branches. It can help to bend the knees to gain a more horizontal chopping action.

You should position yourself so that the branches you are striking with the axe are either in front of you or farther forward in the strike. Put another way, you do not want the branches you are cutting to be between you and the axe, with the follow-through after the cut carrying the axe toward you. The follow-through after the axe strikes the branch should be past you. This can be achieved in a number of ways. You can stand so that you swing the axe horizontally past you in a forehand motion, with the strike in front of you or slightly past you and the follow-through of the axe being past you. Or you can turn so you are cutting backward, with the strike to your side, and follow through behind. The latter is much more easily effected with the axe in one hand.

With a good-quality axe, well maintained and sharp, you can cut through branches of significant size with one cut. You do need to be committed, though, and positioning of your body for safety is paramount. For thicker branches that cannot be chopped with one cut, start with a couple of cuts to create a V notch, then cut through from the back of the V.

1. *Reasonably sized branches of up to a couple of inches in diameter can easily be removed with one swift, clean cut.*

2. *Tackling a larger branch, I again have positioned my body behind the point the axe will strike.*

3. *The strike point is just ahead of being in line with my hip. Another more downward cut will remove a V-shaped chunk of wood from the branch, so I can take it off with the following cut.*

4. *And with a definitive, near-horizontal strike with an axe, the branch—here in midair—is removed. The follow-through with the axe is past my body.*

Sectioning Considerations

Unless the tree is quite small, once you have removed its branches, you'll need to section it into smaller pieces to move it. When I am winter camping in the boreal forest, I tend to cut the dead wood I have felled into sections as long as I can physically carry on my shoulder, then take them back one by one to where the tent is pitched. There the wood can be further processed by my buddies and me, down to a size that will fit into the woodburning stove in the tent. It's an obvious point, but have a think about the end use of the wood before you go hacking it into short sections. You need to think not only about the required lengths for the end use, but also where knots, kinks, and other imperfections are located.

While I am going to discuss sectioning with an axe, it should be mentioned right from the top that in certain circumstances this can be much less efficient than using a suitable saw. Axes are good chopping and splitting tools. They work particularly well along or at a slight angle to the grain. They cut much less well across the grain. Saws, on the other hand, cut well across the grain. Further, to cut through a log with an axe you have to waste more wood than with a saw. That said, saws can easily get stuck in logs if they become pinched in the cut. Equally, saw blades of shallow depth will tend to wander as soon as they go even a little bit off line. This can cause the saw to jam too. Finally, if you don't have a saw with you, or if you don't have a saw big enough to tackle the diameter of wood, then the axe is your only choice. As you can imagine from the techniques shown earlier in this chapter, it's certainly possible to fell a tree with axe and saw but for the trunk of the tree to be too thick to section with the very same saw. This is because the felling job does not require you to saw through the whole trunk, only the part of trunk that remains at the back of the tree after you have made a front cut with the axe. So there are a number of reasons why sectioning with an axe is a skill you should have in your repertoire.

Open Wide and Remove Chunks

To cut through a trunk with an axe, you need to make the cut much wider than the cut made by a saw. To this extent, you will waste more wood than if sectioning with a saw. The rule of thumb for sectioning with an axe is to open up a cut that is as wide as the diameter of the trunk. This allows you to remove wood quickly from the trunk, and

then, when around halfway through, you can switch sides and bring the cut into the middle from the other side of the trunk.

A common mistake is to try to cut into a narrow V. Cutting into the apex of any V cut with an axe is inefficient. Instead, you should aim to remove chunks of wood by methodically and progressively working an area with the axe, altering the angle somewhat to encourage the wood to fire out of the cut.

1. *Standing behind the log I am about to section. I will attack it on the opposite side to my legs with the axe.*

2. *Depending on the length of the axe, you may need to bend your knees or your back (or both) so the axe strikes the trunk squarely, rather than glancing over the top toward your legs.*

3. The rule of thumb is to cut out a notch as wide as the diameter of the tree.

4. Chunking out a notch to section a small tree. Note the chunks flying out of the cut.

5. Chunks of wood removed by efficient and effective axe work.

6. It continues to be easy to remove material from the base of the notch when it is this wide.

7. Chunking out wood from the notch on the log at ground level, using a larger axe.

8. Note the spacing between where the axe has cut. This allows chunks of wood to be removed in one go.

9. Once about halfway through or a little more, move to the other side of the log and continue as before.

10. Getting close to being all the way through here. Just throttle back on the power so you have a little more control. A couple more cuts and it will be through and on the same side of the log as your legs.

11. The final cut. Note where the axe is relative to the log. Also note how one end of the cut log has fallen and the other has risen.

8

10

9

11

Felling, Limbing, and Sectioning

Ambidextrous Axe Usage

Most right-handed people are happy to use an axe left-handed, and they don't even realize it. Equally, left-handed people are happy to use an axe right-handed and don't realize they are doing so. When swinging an axe, most people tend to lift the head with their dominant hand and hold their nondominant hand at the end of the handle to guide the axe. It's relatively easy to learn to use it the other way around, too, since all you are doing is learning to guide with your dominant hand. To understand this, it's first easier to deconstruct the action and think about chopping using only one hand to hold the axe.

1. *Right hand (my dominant) lifting the head, left hand guiding the swing from the back.*

2. *Left hand lifting the head, right hand guiding from the back.*

3. *Right-handed use of the axe with two hands. Left hand is guiding at the rear.*

Learning to use the axe ambidextrously allows you to attack at all the angles you need to create a symmetrical cut and remove material quickly and easily by changing the angle of attack from left to right and right to left. When using a larger axe, it's even more important. If you can learn to use the axe ambidextrously, not only is your technique more efficient, it's also better for your back in the long run. Not many people bother to learn this or even know about it, but it is well worth the effort.

4. *Left-handed use of the axe with two hands. Right hand is guiding at the rear.*

5. *Chopping with my right (dominant) hand holding the axe.*

6. *Chopping with my left hand holding the axe.*

7. *This is awkward, and I am twisting my back. It's due to the hand positioning, which is the opposite of how it should be to attack from the left.*

8. *Comfortably swinging the axe, accurately guiding with my left hand.*

9. *The beginning of the switch. Just after the axe has stopped, I start to remove my previously guiding left hand while gripping the handle with my right.*

10. *My left hand now slides forward into position to lift the head of the axe.*

11. *At the top of the lift and about to swing down again. My right hand is now guiding, the opposite of the previous swing, and I can comfortably swing the axe from left to right.*

12. *At the bottom of the swing. My hands are the opposite to the previous downward swing, and the angle of attack is angled in from the other side. I can do this without twisting my back or other awkwardness.*

4

5

6

Splitting Long Logs

You may have noticed that as pieces of firewood on your chopping block increase in length, they become harder to split, other things being equal. Also, when you are splitting wood to create the starting pieces for one or more carving projects, you require more control of the split than provided by the dynamic axe swing suitable for splitting firewood.

Similarly, when we are splitting longer logs, especially if we need them for a project around camp, we need to take a different approach again. If we have metal splitting wedges and a splitting maul, the solution is relatively easy, as well as obvious.

Using metal splitting wedges to first create, then continue a split along a log

If we don't have a splitting maul and wedges but only a half-length general-purpose axe, or even a three-quarter axe, what do we do? Well, we have to make some tools first. We'll need some wooden wedges, known traditionally as gluts. We'll also need some sort of wooden mallet. We'll look at how to make these later in this chapter, but first let's look at how we split a long log by using them. This will not only show you the technique but also give you some context for what is being made in the next couple of sections.

1. *These are the tools we use to split longer logs when we have no specialist equipment, only our general-purpose axe and an improvised mallet and wooden gluts.*

2. *Start by using your axe to remove the bark from the log along the line you wish to split it.*

3. *Next, hammer the axe into the end grain of the log, using the improvised mallet. This will initiate a longitudinal split.*

4. *Next, hammer one of the gluts into the split just beyond the axe.*

5. *As the glut enters the wood, it does two things: it increases the split and it loosens the wood's hold on the axe.*

6. *As the axe loosens, remove it. It could be handy for other jobs during the splitting process. If you can get a glut into the split beyond the first, then do so. If not, get one in behind it so they can work in tandem.*

7. *The aim of the game from here on is to use one glut to increase the split sufficiently so you can progress the other glut to increase the split farther along, either shuffling them forward or leapfrogging them.*

8. *An important aspect of this is listening. You will hear the wood fibers relaxing and giving way. Hammer the gluts, then pause to listen. If you try to progress too quickly, the split may run off where you don't want it to. To this end, also keep an eye on the progress of the split in the area where you removed the bark.*

9. *If you are patient and methodical, eventually the log will split.*

10. *You would not be able to split this log with only your forest axe. But with some tools you can make with your forest axe, you can then split the log.*

1

2

3

4

5

6

7

8

9

10

Making Gluts

To make our wooden wedges, or gluts, we are going to employ axe-carving techniques covered in detail in chapter 5 (page 139). If you are unfamiliar with basic carving techniques with an axe, then I would highly recommend you review the relevant sections of chapter 5 before embarking on making some gluts. As well as being safe, you also want to have good technique. Gluts are best made from hardwoods at the hard end of the spectrum. In a northern temperate context, we mean the likes of holly or hornbeam, for example. These will, of course, be relatively hard work to carve, even green. Holly has the advantage of being quite waxy when green, which at least anecdotally seems to help with getting the glut established into a crack in the wood.

You will need at least two gluts. There is nothing to stop you from making three or four just in case you need them. Moreover, for very long splits or particularly tough or knotty wood, you will likely need more than two. It's easy to carve gluts in pairs, though, so I would suggest going for two or four to start with.

1. *Start with a piece of wood for your gluts that is at least the length of two gluts, then start carving a long taper from near the center to the end.*

2. *Pace yourself, since hard hardwoods are by definition difficult to carve. Also make sure your tapers are not skewed or twisted relative to each other.*

3. *Once you have two flat surfaces converging at the end of the log, bring them together into a fine edge by creating a secondary bevel.*

4. *Also chamfer the sides slightly, since this will help prolong the life of the gluts by reducing the chances of the edges fraying or splitting away. The overall effect you are aiming for at the tip is akin to a screwdriver.*

5. *Once you have one end completed, repeat the process at the other end.*

6. *When you have two completed tapers, with chamfers, cut the piece in half, creating two separate wedges.*

7. *Now bevel the ends like a tent peg to help prevent the glut from splitting when struck by a mallet or axe poll.*

8. *The finished article.*

9. *Two gluts ready to go. Now we need a mallet.*

1

2

3

4

5

6

7

8

9

Making a Woodland Mallet

The aim here is to make something hefty yet wieldy. It's something with which we will be able to strike our axe without distorting the eye, as well as hammering gluts into wood we want to split. This is not rocket science by any means, but there is a little knack and judgment involved in getting this right. The drawback of getting it wrong is pretty low, though, since these don't take long to make and if you mess it up, you can quickly have another go and likely get it right.

1. Start by sourcing a straight piece of timber that is knot free for about 18 in. (45 cm) and so won't be horrible to split. I tend to use green timber, since it will be heavier due to the moisture content.

2. Mark, mentally or physically, where the end of the mallet will be.

3. Saw into the wood roughly halfway along its intended length, between the mark and the end.

4. Keep your cut parallel to the ground and stop at least an inch (2.5 cm) short of the center of the wood.

5

5. Rotate the wood by 90 degrees and make another cut the same as before, stopping short of the center. Then repeat this process twice more so you have made four cuts in total, all of them stopping short of the center by at least an inch (2.5 cm).

6. Now saw the piece off at the original end marker, not in the middle where your four cuts are.

7. Place the round on a block, with the end you'd like to be the handle facing upward.

8. Place your axe on one side of the center, about an inch (2.5 cm) away from the middle.

6

8

7

9. Baton the side off down to the stop cut you sawed. Be careful not to split beyond the stop cut.

10. Rotate the piece 90 degrees, then split the side off.

11. After rotating by a right angle and splitting off the side twice more, your piece should look something like this.

12. Now split off the square edges of the center stalk that will be the handle of the mallet.

13. After splitting off the final square corner, you should end up with a handle that is octagonal.

14. Taking your knife, shave off any edges that aren't comfortable in the hand, and make sure the handle is not too big for your hand. If so, reduce it by shaving around and keeping the handle as central as possible.

15. Final touches to the handle.

16. Now you have all of your splitting equipment.

These mallets last a long time and are useful for other jobs, including hitting a froe when making shingles or chopping boards, or even just hitting large tent pegs into the ground.

9

10

11

Carving Techniques and Projects

Knife Safety

Knife safety starts with choosing the right knife for the job. Folding knives are handy in the outdoors but have an inherent weakness at the hinge. A knife with a fixed blade will be stronger than a folding knife, even a locking folder. With a fixed blade there is no chance of it folding on your fingers. In choosing a fixed-blade knife, you should also select one with a strong sheath. This protects both you and your knife.

Taking a knife out of its sheath

The thing to remember is to keep your fingers away from the cutting edge of a knife when unsheathing it. Familiarize yourself with your knife so you know which side the cutting edge will emerge.

Be aware of where the cutting edge of your knife is.

WRONG: Where not to put your fingers when unsheathing a knife.

Keep your fingers well out of the way.

When you are not using your knife, put it back in the sheath. The safest place for your knife is in its sheath. Don't be tempted to stick it in a log or a tree stump for a few minutes or otherwise leave it lying around. With plenty of potential trip hazards outdoors, you should replace your knife in its sheath before walking even a short distance. You could cause yourself or others serious injury if you fall with a knife in your hand.

Put your knife safely back in its sheath when you are not using it.

Give yourself and others room

Don't try to use your knife in awkward or confined spaces. Give yourself enough room to use it properly.

When using your knife, make sure you leave enough room around you so that you don't endanger other people. If someone is within arm's reach, they are too close.

Be aware

If you are using a knife, be aware of the movement of other people around you. They may not have noticed you are using a knife.

Be aware of others using knives. If someone is using a knife nearby, make sure you stay at a safe distance. Don't rush around near someone using a knife.

Concentrate on what you are doing

Many cuts are due to a lack of concentration, either due to distractions or tiredness. If you aren't able to concentrate, put your knife away until you can.

Hold your knife securely

Make sure you have a secure grip on the knife. The basic grip is the forehand grip. This and other grips are covered in more detail later in this chapter.

Cut away from yourself

Cut away from your body and cut away from your limbs. Pay particular attention to the position of the hand that is not holding the knife.

Do not cut toward the supporting hand, even if most of it is on the other side of the workpiece.

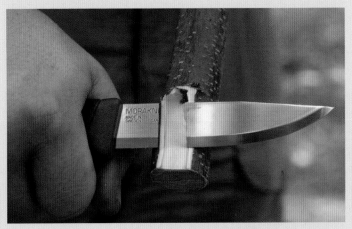

Remove modest amounts of material in a controlled action.

If you need more power, work on the outside of your body and generate power by dropping your shoulder.

Cutting away from the body and from the supporting hand. This is safe.

Don't be overambitious

Even with a sharp knife, aim to shave off modest amounts of material with each cut of the knife. Trying to remove excessive amounts of wood with each cut will require excessive force, leading to tired hand muscles and reduced control of the knife.

Safely create extra power by holding the piece like this, then dropping the shoulder.

If you need more stability, work onto a log, tree stump, or chopping block. Just be careful that you don't bash your knuckles.

For extra support, work onto a stable wooden block or log. Note I'm also working on the outside of my body, and my legs are well out of the way.

Elbows on knees

Your major arteries run along the insides of your limbs. This means these blood vessels are vulnerable if you use a knife toward these areas. Cutting the major artery in a leg—the femoral artery—is potentially fatal, so take special care not to use a knife in a way that risks this. A particular concern is carving while sitting down. This brings your legs up closer to your hands, so you need to be careful while using a knife. Keeping your elbows on your knees prevents the knife coming close to your leg.

WRONG: Don't allow yourself to work with the knife close to your inner thigh.

Think about where the knife will go if you slip

For every cut you make with your knife, consider where it will go next—not only if things go to plan, but also if you slip, or if you cut straight through what you are working on. Position yourself so that the next thing your knife hits isn't you.

WRONG: A slip with the knife here is potentially lethal.

The right way to do it. Working with elbows on knees forces your hands away from your thighs and your knife away from your femoral arteries.

Listen to the sensible voice in your head

If you feel like you are using your knife in a way that is risky or foolish, then you probably are. Listen to the voice in your head (or funny feeling in your gut) telling you so. Then alter what you are doing so it is safe. If you can't figure out a way of safely achieving what you would like, ask someone with more experience for some direction.

Keep your knife sharp

It may seem counterintuitive, but a sharp knife is a safe knife. A sharp knife is predictable. You don't need to apply excessive force. The knife cuts in a familiar way, and you easily achieve what you need to.

Knife Grips

Having a variety of knife grips allows you to call on a full range of cutting strokes, which in turn opens up a world of crafting opportunities. Just as a bad workman blames his tools, a good workman gets the most out of even simple tools. There's a joy to watching someone achieving much with little, never mind achieving it oneself. The grips in this section lead directly to a range of carving techniques covered in the next section and are put into practice throughout this book.

The Forehand Grip

The forehand grip is the most intuitive knife grip. It is used for holding the knife while pushing or slicing the knife away from the body, for pushing down onto a block, or in some reinforced knife strokes. Note the thumb is not, as a matter of course, placed on the back of the blade while taking up this grip. Make a fist around the handle, with your thumb wrapped around the handle too.

The basic forehand grip. The essence of this is to make a fist around the knife handle.

The forehand grip in use, with the knife being pushed while the workpiece is held freehand.

The Backhand Grip

In terms of what your hand does around the knife handle, the backhand grip is essentially the same as the forehand grip. The difference is the knife is rotated 180 degrees around its longitudinal axis, so the cutting edge is facing the web of your hand rather than away from it. The backhand grip is used when you are pulling the edge toward the body and in some reinforced strokes.

The backhand grip. This puts the cutting edge of the knife facing the web of the hand.

Backhand grip in use as the author performs a pull stroke with a carving knife.

The Side Grip

Somewhere between the forehand grip and the backhand grip is the side grip. It can be oriented with the cutting edge of the knife facing away from the fingers or toward them. The latter can sometimes be used as part of a chest lever stroke (see page 138), or as a gentle finishing stroke while carving.

The Blade Grip

In this grip the blade is strangled by the knife hand, with the knife being held at least partially on the blade. It should be obvious that one does not wrap the fingers around the sharp cutting edge. This grip usually brings the thumb down the side of the knife, with some of the blade protruding farther. In some ways it is like using a shorter-bladed knife.

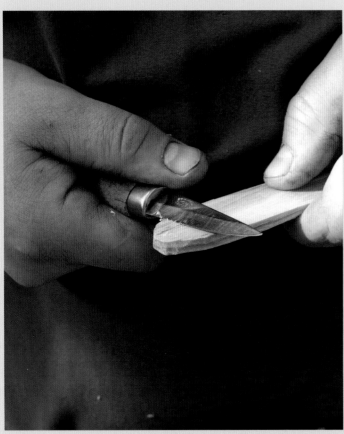

Side grip in use as the knife is used in a planing action to improve the finish.

Blade grip in use, effectively shortening the blade.

Carving Techniques for a Knife

The carving techniques we employ with a knife—the actual cutting strokes we make—build on the foundation of our knife grips.

Supporting Your Work

While much of our carving might be done freehand, it is useful at times to be able to support the work. This can be either for reasons of safety or for the purpose of controlling the way that wood is removed from the workpiece. A simple example is supporting the piece on a stump or a log while pushing down its length with a knife held in a forehand grip. Quite a lot of force can be applied, and the surface is effectively planed rather than scalloped, the latter being more likely when the piece is held freehand.

The forehand grip being applied in a forceful yet controlled downward stroke, with the workpiece being supported on a log.

Here a lighter push stroke is being applied to bring this spatula to a smooth finish. The firm footing provided by supporting the piece on a chopping block allows for consistent application of the stroke, as well as being able to work right to the edge of the spatula.

Cutting Toward Yourself

It may seem contradictory to our general knife safety guidelines, but when carving there are times when you might want to draw the knife toward you. It's important for your safety that you do this by pulling the handle of the knife toward your body, rather than pushing the blade toward your body. You cannot stab yourself with the handle. At the same time, you must make sure the blade is moving away from the supporting hand.

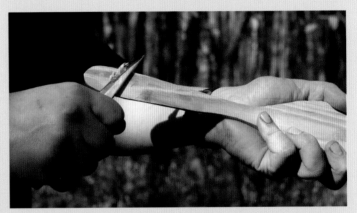

Using the backhand grip, here the knife is being drawn handle-first toward the body (and away from the supporting hand).

Here more of a side grip is being used. With the thumb on the blade, and the edge locked in at a set angle against the wood, the rest of the thumb acts as a guide for a plane-like movement as the knife is drawn handle-first toward the body.

The Chest Hold

Sometimes it is efficacious to employ the chest hold, particularly for allowing a planing action with the knife on straight edges or for creating internal curves. The workpiece is then effectively clamped between your sternum and your nonknife hand. This is often used in combination with a backhand grip and moving the knife toward the body.

This is a variant of the chest hold. The handle of the workpiece is still being supported on the sternum even though the grip and cutting stroke of the knife have changed to move away from the body. Note that the supporting hand has been moved to a safe position behind the blade.

In the chest hold, the workpiece is clamped between the supporting hand and the sternum, providing a solid platform on which to work.

The Squeeze Grip

This could be considered a type of reinforced backhand grip, since the thumb of the knife hand is employed to gain extra purchase and control. I think it is worth exploring as a distinct technique, though, especially since the cutting edge of the knife is moving toward your knife hand. Here, the important safety point is that the blade is not squeezed toward the thumb. Rather, the knife handle is squeezed toward the web of the knife hand, so the blade goes past the thumb, not into it.

A partial blade grip being used to bring the curved part of a general-purpose knife to bear to create an internal curve. The chest hold provides a stable platform.

Here using the squeeze grip with a carving knife. Note that the edge of the knife is not being moved toward the thumb. Rather, the handle of the knife is being squeezed toward the web of the hand, taking the cutting edge to the side of the thumb.

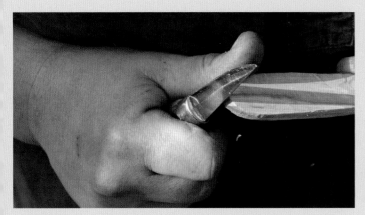

The knife moves to the side of the thumb, not toward it.

In this reinforced grip, the reinforcing thumb is being used as something of a pivot point.

Reinforced Grips

Reinforced grips are standard grips reinforced by extra contact with the knife, usually but not necessarily from a thumb. This can be to create extra leverage, but it is often to facilitate a greater degree of control.

In this reinforced grip, the index finger of the nonknife hand is being used as a pivot point while the rest of the hand holds the piece in place.

The cut is being reinforced here by placing an additional thumb on the back of the knife near to the tip, which also increases control.

Side grip in use with reinforcement from the thumb of the hand holding the workpiece to remove material from around the edge of a shallow spoon.

A good degree of controlled force is required to cut across the grain of seasoned wood. Here, a forehand grip is being reinforced by the thumb of the hand holding the workpiece, which is acting to create a type of squeeze grip, as well as a pivot point for added leverage.

Side grip in use with reinforcement from the fingers of the other hand.

Chest lever stroke being used to remove the remains of a side branch.

The Chest Lever

The chest lever is a powerful yet highly controlled knife stroke. The knife is either in the backhand grip or side grip, depending on what you are working on. The knife always travels horizontally, never up or down toward the body. The workpiece is locked in position by the supporting hand and sometimes clamped under the arm too. The knife moves by being pulled through the wood. Don't think about pushing the knife with your hand. Think about pulling with your arm, with the pull coming from your elbow. Indeed, you can move both elbows in opposite directions. You are using the muscles between the shoulder blades, with a sort of chicken wing action with your arms to create the power yet maintain control.

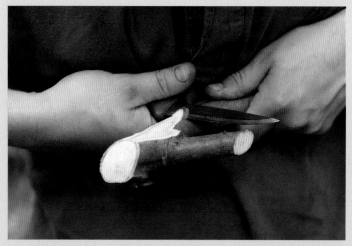

Backhand grip in use as part of a chest lever stroke. The blade is cutting away from the body and the nonknife hand.

Carving Techniques and Projects

Carving Techniques with a General-Purpose Axe

Carving with an axe speeds up projects you could potentially complete with a knife. Carving with an axe also opens up the possibility of undertaking projects you would not contemplate attempting with only a knife. Similar to the techniques for carving with a knife, there are some core grips and concepts to grasp here. Everything here takes the safety points in chapter 3 (pages 60–66) as read. When carving with an axe, you can work on a high or low chopping block, or even a horizontal log on the ground. Make sure you are standing or kneeling as appropriate.

Batoning with an Axe

We have a range of splitting techniques that lend themselves to quickly paring down lumps of firewood. When it comes to starting a carving project, though, we need a little more precision than swinging the axe typically permits. So we will place the axe where we want the split to start, then hit the poll of the axe with a log or similar wooden baton with sufficient weight to drive the axe into the wood.

1. *Place the axe bit where you want the split to start, then tap with the wooden baton.*

2. *Hit the poll of the axe with the baton with sufficient force to begin to drive the axe into the wood. Try to keep the handle horizontal.*

3. *When the piece finally splits, be mindful of where the axe goes next. Remember to follow the core safety principles (see chapter 3).*

Axe-Carving Grips

The best general-purpose axes for carving are hatchets and half axes. Three-quarter and larger felling axes are too unwieldy for carving due to the length of their handles. Even so, when using smaller axes you need to vary your grip a fair amount, from gripping way down the handle to strangling the handle right behind the head. Sometimes you may even take your hand up onto and around the back of the head and the poll. The farther back toward the swell of the handle you hold the axe, the more chop it will have, but the less control you will maintain. This is good for removing lots of material quickly but is not great for finer work. As you move your hand toward the head, you will decrease the radius of the arc on which the head travels, and there will be increased dampening of the swing from the portion of the handle behind the hand. As you bring your hand right up behind the head and fully strangle the axe, there is less leverage still, but greater control again. The swing now needs to come from the wrist rather than the elbow. Moving the hand farther forward still, you are into the realm of no swing at all, rather using the axe as a heavy knife in more of a push cut than an axe swing.

1. *Holding the axe in the middle of the handle allows a good amount of chop, but also good control. Here a significant amount of the movement originates at the elbow.*

2. *Bringing your hand up closer to the head means more control, but by moving the elbow a good amount of cutting ability is still available.*

3. *A grip close to the head also allows you to do relatively fine work.*

4. *The axe is fully strangled for smaller, more controlled cuts.*

5. *Viewed from this perspective, you can see that the workpiece is angled to keep the axe working vertically.*

6. *Here the axe is held even farther up the head. The author's finger is laid down the side of the axe bit, which also helps with increased control and a lighter cut with the axe. Almost all the movement is coming from the wrist.*

7. *A similar grip here, but now working across the grain in a planing action that utilizes the axe more as a heavy knife.*

8. *Even working on a low log, it is possible to use a controlled carving technique and observe core safety principles.*

Spoon Knives and Their Use

A spoon knife is the missing link of basic carving. You can get only so far with knife, saw, and axe. Add a spoon knife into your limited toolkit, however, and you have the ability to form a bowl—and quickly create well-finished eating spoons, other similar larger utensils, and deeper bowls, such as ladles and cups.

Spoon knives have curved blades.

A spoon knife has a curved blade and is thus either right-handed or left-handed. A right-handed spoon knife curves to the left, and a left-handed spoon knife curves to the right. A further distinction is that spoon knives have only a single bevel. This bevel is on the outside of the curve, with the inside of the curve having no bevel. The spoon knife works something like an ice cream scoop. Unlike ice cream, though, wood has grain.

Spoon knives have a single bevel on the outside of the curve of the blade.

In terms of adding a spoon knife to your carving kit, go for a standard-sized spoon knife first. There is no real stated, agreed-on standard, but many makers make a small spoon knife, which is their de facto standard spoon knife that will be suitable for making small spoons of the type you would eat with, up to medium-sized spoons. A larger-diameter spoon knife is suited to larger spoons. I would recommend that you choose a spoon knife that is handed for your dominant hand, rather than purchase one of the double-edged knives that are often attractive to the frugal beginner. These double-edged knives can cause a disproportionate number of cuts to the hands of users.

It's worth a reminder at this stage that we are not equipping ourselves with a full green woodworking tool set. We are coming at the skills and tools from the perspective of what can be made on the trail, either with a very lightweight set of tools or in a temporary camp, perhaps with a few more tools, but which will still be quite general purpose. We are not going to have access to a full set of straight and bent woodcarving gouges, for example.

By adding a standard spoon knife to a general-purpose woodcraft knife, you can easily turn out very respectable spoons.

The basic tool set that will allow anyone to complete the majority of the woodcarving projects featured in this book includes a general-purpose axe, a general-purpose knife, and a spoon knife. Specialist tools help save time and effort and allow a greater degree of finesse in the end product. The itinerant woodcrafter, however, needs to have as their baseline of skill an ability to make what they need with a very limited range of tools.

Using a Spoon Knife

The directions that follow are based on good practice and having observed the common mistakes many times. After picking up a spoon knife, the main incidents you want to avoid are cutting yourself or ruining your carving project.

Wood varies from species to species. Some are very fine grained, while others are very coarse. Wherever on this spectrum the material you are carving sits, if you are carving a spoon bowl you will need to be careful not to pull wood fibers out of where you want the bowl and mess up the finish of the surrounding area of the utensil. For this reason, I recommend you largely work across the grain, especially as you first establish your bowl. This allows you to cut the fibers cleanly, rather than lifting the fibers, and this lift running outside your bowl area.

In terms of how to hold the spoon knife to achieve the cross-grain cut, you should adopt a similar grip to the squeeze grip (see page 136). The important similarity is that you should bring the handle of the spoon knife to the web of your hand, not bring the knife to your thumb; otherwise you will end up with an irritating crescent-shaped cut on your digit.

Generally you should be using a spoon knife that is handed for your dominant hand. So, being right-handed, I use a right-handed spoon knife for most of my spoon bowl carving. Start by cutting across and into the grain. Make a series of intersecting cuts to begin to establish one side of the bowl. Then turn the workpiece 180 degrees and undertake the same process with the same spoon knife on the other side of the bowl.

Once you begin to achieve some depth to the bowl, you can begin to scoop around at each end of your initial cuts in order to gain the curvature of the bowl you require. Cutting this way reduces your chances of lifting fibers out of the area where you want to achieve the bowl.

1. *Start by cutting across the grain. Place your thumb on the workpiece, opposite to the cutting edge, and use your fingers to squeeze the spoon knife handle toward the web of your hand, rather than bringing the edge toward your thumb.*

2. *Work with a spoon knife handed for your dominant hand, supporting the piece with your other hand.*

3. *Turn the piece through 180 degrees to work from the other side of the bowl, rather than using an opposite-handed spoon knife.*

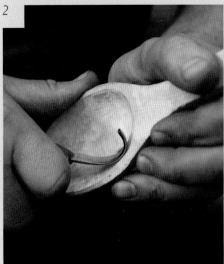

4. Once you have started to form your bowl, you can begin to scallop around the ends of the bowl, rather than only working perpendicular to the grain. This is only a shallow spoon, but the principle remains the same regardless of the depth.

5. Once you have some depth to the bowl, you can work more along the grain with less risk.

6. As the bowl begins to be more defined, you can cut from the end of the bowl, along the grain, rather than just across it. Start by cutting down into the bowl to cut the ends of the grain, then reduce the angle and cut along the bowl, removing material as you go.

7. Here I'm working along the grain at the edge of the bowl. Note how the less curved part of the spoon knife blade is being utilized here. Remember to scallop the cut around more across the grain toward the end of the spoon, rather than lifting fibers or chipping the edge of the bowl.

Creating Wooden Utensils

With a repertoire of carving techniques you can carve useful utensils for the camp, from small eating spoons to larger utensils such as spatulas, serving spoons, ladles, and even cups. It's a wonderful sense of accomplishment to make a set of utensils that you'll use and care for. You can make them to the specifications you want in terms of size, function, and robustness. The required techniques come from the knife grips and axe techniques already described in this chapter, utilizing these core components, building on them in places, and using them in creative ways.

Right: *A range of utensils carved by the author from wild cherry.*

Carving Spatulas

As a carving project, a spatula has a lot going for it in terms of improving your carving technique. A spatula is a less complex shape than a spoon, but it requires all of the basic axe- and knife-carving techniques you will use on just about any project, save for using a spoon knife to create a bowl. A spatula requires a starting piece of wood too thick to split with your knife, so you will have to employ an axe to split the round. You can then continue with the axe in hewing the shape of the spatula. My challenge to you is to see how far you can go with forming a spatula before you have to resort to using a knife. This will really help improve your carving skill with an axe, especially if you are relatively new to using an axe this way.

1. *Split the piece by batoning your axe.*

2. *Create a good baseline flat surface on the inside of the half you are using.*

3. *Once you are happy you have a good baseline on the inside of the split part, remove the sap wood from the outside of the piece. The aim here is to create a surface parallel to your baseline.*

4. Next draw around a card template or an actual spatula.

5. Now start carving down to the lines you have drawn as a guide.

6. Here I'm working as far down the grain as I can before turning the piece to come at it from the other end.

7. Having turned the piece, I bring the curve down to meet the fibers I removed from the handle end and so remove them.

8. Next I work on the shape at the end of the spatula blade.

9. Note the axe is strangled here, and the taps with the axe are light as I move to cutting more across the grain.

10. With the end shape of the spatula cut out, I now further thin down its blade.

11. Reducing the leading edge of the spatula.

12. You can work across the grain with a sharp axe, further flattening the surface.

13. Assessing what else needs to be done. So far, this has all been achieved with a general-purpose half axe.

14. Further refining the blade of the spatula, using the axe as a heavy knife.

15. This is already a useable spatula, carved entirely with an axe. If I so desire, I could continue to refine this with my knife. See below for how you might apply the knife.

10

13

11

14

12

15

The author about to serve a meal cooked over a campfire with utensils he previously carved himself. (Photo by Ray Goodwin)

Carving Larger Spoons

Carving larger spoons is an extension of the same. Indeed, if you progress through carving small eating spoons with a knife, then introduce the axe on further examples before moving on to larger objects such as spatulas with the axe, then you'll have a good foundation of technique for making larger spoons. Large spoons are useful in your camp kitchen set for mixing, stirring, and serving.

If you want to make a relatively straight spoon with a deeper bowl, then start with a half round of wood that is deep enough to accommodate the depth of bowl below the level of the handle. If you want a significant crank in the spoon, with an angle between the top of the bowl and the handle, the handle will rise more above the level of the bowl. In this case you have two options. The first choice is to find a thicker piece of wood. Your second is to select a piece of wood that isn't necessarily as thick but has the requisite

curvature already, which will yield the shape of spoon you want. This latter option has the added advantage of the grain matching the shape of the spoon and thus providing additional strength. If you wish to progress to deep serving spoons with curved handles or ladles, then you must start looking at sections of trees with side branches at the desired angle. The bowl can be carved from the main body of the tree, while the handle is formed from part of the side branch.

Large, shapely spoons are quite a lot of work and can be daunting for the beginner. I'd recommend starting with carving a shallow spoon, because it is one step beyond the spatula and also consolidates what you've learned already. The way you get to the roughed-out shape is exactly as with the spatula. We can now look at how we can use the knife and the spoon knife to finish the job.

In some ways the early shaping of a spoon or spatula is quite mechanical. There are stages you go through in a process that results in a shape that is hewn from the wood, more or less the shape and size in plane and in elevation that will progress to being the object you are aiming to produce. Once you get down to this shape, though, the process is a little more free form. The aim is to refine the overall piece by reducing bumps and blemishes, by smoothing surfaces and curves, removing edges where you don't want them and adding definition where you do. Some like to finish their pieces only with a knife, not using any abrasive paper or similar to further smooth the piece. This requires a sharp knife, a good eye, and deft control of the knife, making definitive final cuts. Whichever finishing process you go for, note that before this you are working with a unique piece of natural material. Hence, you need to apply your knife-carving techniques in a fluid, flexible way to achieve the shape you want. Following are some of them being applied.

Left: The bowl of this serving spoon was carved by the author from the trunk of a large birch tree, with the handle carved from a side branch emanating from the same tree. This provides the necessary angles as well as an inherent strength.

The basic form of this shallow spoon has been established with an axe.

1. It's time to move over to using the knife and a spoon knife to turn this form into a useable utensil.

2. Bowl to chest, using the chest hold, and planing the edge of the handle with a carving knife in a blade grip.

3. A squeeze grip in use while refining the curve at the front of the spoon.

4. A pull stroke with the knife in a backhand grip while refining the handle.

5. A push stroke with the workpiece supported on a block.

3

1

4

2

5

6. *A pull stroke being used to plane the handle.*

7. *Handle to chest, again using the chest hold, and knife in something between a backhand grip and a side grip.*

8. *A reinforced stroke being used to shape the outside of the bowl.*

9. *Side grip being combined with a light-touch chest lever arrangement to take material from the bottom of a shallow spoon bowl.*

10. *Forming the bowl of a shallow spoon.*

11. *Using fingers and thumbs as a gauge of thickness to guide where to remove more material from the spoon bowl.*

12. *The finished shallow spoon with the tools used to finish it.*

The above principles can be extended to deeper spoons with relatively straight handles. The key with deeper spoons, with larger bowls carved from a greater mass of wood, is not to leave the material in the bowl area too long before removing it. As you split and further expose the wood to air by carving away the outer layers, it will dry out quite quickly. This is not an issue for a relatively slender and flexible handle, but a solid bowl area full of wood will begin to warp and crack if left as a solid lump. Hence some carvers like to remove this material before finishing other aspects of the spoon, particularly if they are working outdoors in warm, dry air. Indeed, removing the bowl material before the rest of the spoon is completed does allow you to put down the project, then return to it later with less risk of it being ruined.

13. *Tidying up the finish on a spoon bowl that had been hollowed out some weeks before.*

6

7

8

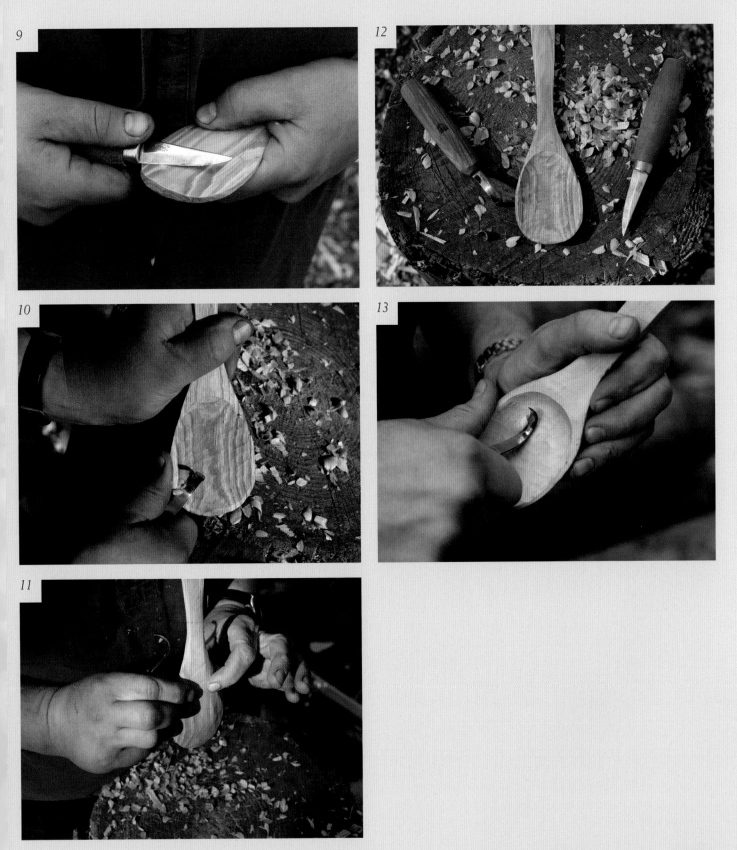

Finishing Your Projects

Knife finish or sanded? Even though each woodcarver has their opinion and preference, there is no universally right or wrong answer. As well as being a matter of aesthetic values, there are also the questions of function, durability, and hygiene. If I am making a serving spoon to go into a kitchen kit that will be used—and cleaned—by a range of colleagues and students, I'm going to make a much more plain and smooth-surfaced item than an ornate display piece might feature. I want something that is going to be relatively impervious to water, that will not break easily, that will not hold food in little nooks and crannies, and will be easy to keep clean, as well as easy to re-oil as necessary.

Sanding Materials

Sandpaper will render a smooth surface, but it can also remove all that hard-won hand-carved definition you have created with your own fair hands. Don't use sanding as a crutch to support or cover up sloppy carving. Sanding should be used to achieve something you can't with the axe or knife. Even so, I'd recommend not oversanding your pieces, particularly around the edges; otherwise they look somewhat blurry and out of focus. After all, you can buy utensils like this from the store. In the end, though, it is a matter of preference.

Sandpaper can be used to smooth surfaces on carved projects. Have at least the options of coarse, medium, and fine in your carving kit.

Sandpaper is easily available and inexpensive. I find it doesn't last very long, particularly when sanding curved surfaces. It is also susceptible to water. There is a good alternative for the itinerant woodcrafter, though, something I was put on to by a colleague of mine. Abranet™ is a plastic netting material for sanding. Designed to be used on sanding machines and applicable to a range of materials, we've found it also

works well as a hand-sanding material on spatulas, spoons, cups, and boards. The added advantage is that it is robust and lasts a long time, and if it gets wet outdoors, it doesn't matter. Also when the net clogs a little, just knock the dust from the mesh and the netting is as good as new. In your carving kit you need carry only one sheet of each grade.

Sheets of sanding net, from coarse to fine.

The grades of sanding net I include in my carving kit. 80 is usually too coarse. I typically start with 120 or 180, then finish with 320.

Whether you are using sandpaper or sanding net, wait for your project to dry out before you sand it. In terms of drying, you should not try to dry pieces carved from green wood too quickly. Slow, natural drying is best. Even so, a small piece will dry out in days rather than weeks. You'll get the best results from sanding by working up through the grades, similar to how you sharpen your tools. Beware of coarse, highly aggressive sanding materials. You don't want to reshape the piece, just adjust the finish on the existing shape.

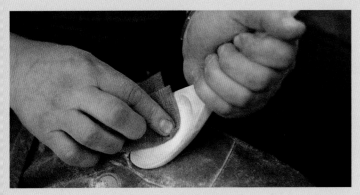

Using sanding netting on the bowl of a large spoon.

Oiling

Once the sanding has been completed, I usually oil utensils, cups, and boards. This helps protect the wood from moisture generally, and foodstuffs in particular. It helps the pieces not to soak in water when cooking or washing, as well as helping limit the flavors they absorb. Personally I usually use walnut oil. It has the advantage of drying after being applied in a thin coat, which means the utensil is not greasy. Nor does the oil go rancid once it is dry. It is food safe, notwithstanding some people's nut allergies.

Walnut oil in small bottles is available from grocery stores.

Other food-safe oils, such as corn oil or olive oil, can be used as an alternative, but they don't dry. Corn oil tends to remain tacky, and olive oil a little greasy. Olive oil is not a particularly resilient finishing oil either, since it tends to be removed by food. If you do use olive oil, then you'll need to reapply the oil fairly regularly if you use the item. Generally you should avoid bringing your wooden utensils into contact with dishwashing soaps and detergents. These chemical agents are designed to break down and remove oils and other grease. You don't want to do this to the finish on your utensils.

Making Things Last

I like to allow a patina of tannins and oil buildup on my small spoons. Such a patina will help seal and protect the wood, increasing the spoon's life span. It also adds to its character. Try to avoid scrubbing your spoon with abrasive pot scrubbers or using too much washing-up detergent, which will remove any oils on the wood. A sponge and warm water or a piece of paper towel should be all you need to clean it without damaging the finish.

A well-used spoon, with a good patina built up on the bowl. The handle is made to be not only comfortable in the hand, but also to fit into the interlocking handles of the mug for safekeeping around camp.

Woodland Campcraft

Quick and Easy Pot Hangers

A simple overnight camp setup including a quick and easy pot hanger.

There are many ways to suspend a pot or a kettle over a fire. Some are simple, some are more complex, some work well on particular types of ground, and others are not so applicable in the same circumstances. Context is king in this respect, and it behooves the outdoors person to have a range of techniques at their disposal, so one of them might fit the circumstances. With all the variants of placing a cooking pot, pan, or kettle over a campfire, I genuinely believe it could be possible to write a book on this subject alone. In my experience, though, some of these methods are more widely applicable and end up being much more commonly used than others.

Further, there are many commonalities between key aspects of the different types of pot hanger, which can be boiled down to a few core concepts. Plus there are certain key techniques, such as the beaked notch (see page 168), that make several suspension methods work. So, it seems to me the best way to equip the reader with a useable arsenal of techniques, without inducing some form of pot hanger overwhelm, is to distill things down. Here I aim to provide methods, partial or complete, that I find useful, and should, in totality, provide a range of techniques sufficient to offer a solution in most circumstances.

First, we should consider the simple, one-stick pot hangers or pot sticks, sometimes referred to as waugun sticks. The origin of this term is mysterious to many. Bernard S. Mason provides a clear explanation of the provenance of this term, though, in *Woodcraft & Camping*: "The simplest and most quickly tossed together device for hanging a kettle is . . . called the wambeck, spygelia or waugun-stick, depending on which part of the northern or eastern woods you are in and the type of native with whom you are talking. The Indians have a word for it in that territory, too—chiplok-wagan or kit-chiplok-wagan, of which waugun-stick is obviously a corruption. This device handles one kettle only and is good for a little lunch fire."

If you can source a stick with a fork in it, then this can be ideal for holding the pot in place, either by hanging the pot on one of the forks, or one of the forks preventing the pot handle slipping down the length of the stick. Before pushing or hammering the stick into the ground, make sure you have ascertained where its stable equilibrium is by allowing it to rotate under its own weight to the point where it wants to rest. Don't force the stick to sit in an orientation it doesn't want to. With slightly curved sticks, the stable equilibrium is usually with the outside of the curve downward. If you position the stick otherwise, then it is prone to rotate once loaded with a pot full of water. This can cause the stick to come unstuck and for you to lose the contents of the pot.

This concept of finding the stable equilibrium has particular relevance if you cannot find a stick with a fork. Then you will need to create a notch in the stick to retain the handle of the pot. If the stick rotates away from where it is first positioned, causing the notch to no longer face upward, it will no longer retain the pot. So first ascertain where the stick wants to sit in stable equilibrium. Then carve a notch into it. We sometimes refer to this style of notch as a crescent notch.

A simple and elegant waugun stick on a lunch fire

Detail of the forked end, cut cleanly and relatively short so as not to impede getting the pot on and off the stick.

The handle of this pot is sitting in a notch carved into the waugun stick, which stops the handle from sliding down the angled stick.

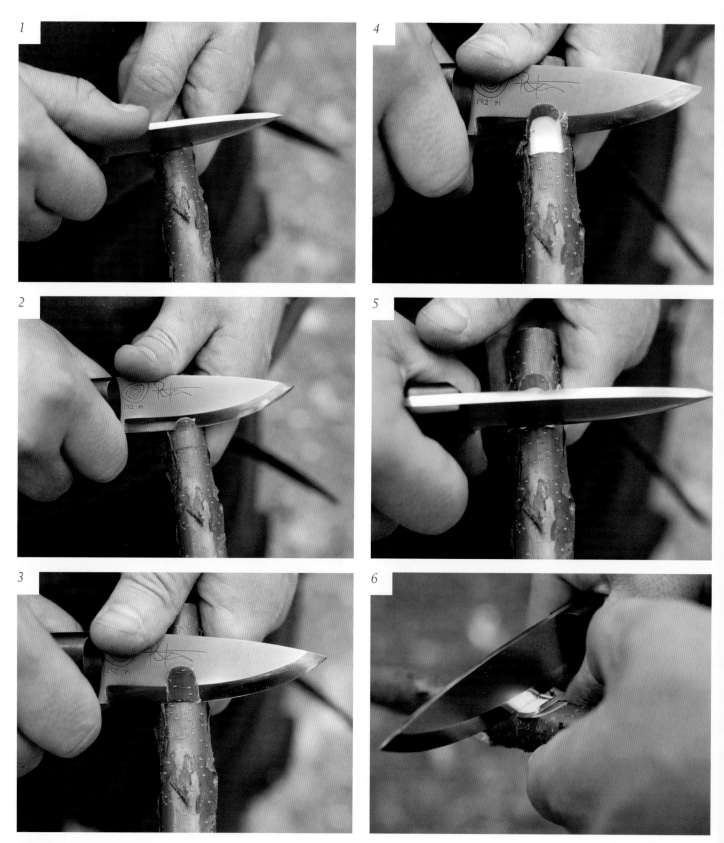

Carving a Crescent Notch

This type of notch is useful for simple wauguns, as well as being used in other areas of campcraft. It's not complicated, but if you are creating this notch close to the end of a stick, you need to be mindful of not cutting yourself.

1. *Take hold of the stick as close to the end as possible while still maintaining a firm grip. Then cut across the stick to start to create a stop cut.*

2. *Slice into and under the bark, working down toward the stop cut.*

3. *At this stage the stop cut is shallow and in soft inner bark. Be careful not to overshoot. Go slow.*

4. *Deepen the stop cut, then slice down to it again.*

5. *Each time deepen the stop cut again.*

6. *Deepening the stop cut also clears previous slices if they are still attached by a few fibers.*

7. *Keep iterating this process. The stop cut will become more solid. You'll be able to remove larger slices with little risk of overshooting the stop cut.*

8. *This is the crescent notch that will retain your pot handle.*

9. *The completed notch seen from the side. Don't cut more than halfway through the diameter of the stick, though, so as not to overly weaken it.*

Supporting the Load

The simplest pot stick is simply just a stick, with the ground being soft enough to accept it but being firm enough that the stick does not cut into the ground when loaded. If the stick does start to drop under the weight of the pot or kettle placed on its end, a solution is to spread the load across the ground, using a second stick, or log, perpendicular to the waugun stick. Or a rock can be used. While introducing support from Y sticks, rocks, and logs can certainly help, it can also lead to an unstable system that is either generally wobbly or sensitive to any sideways movement. This can easily lead to a lost dinner. Equally adding rocks, logs, or other weight to the back of the waugun can help prevent the stick from coming out of the ground or keep it on the ground. But equally, this load can add more force onto whatever is holding up the stick nearer to the fire, which again can lead to increased instability.

A better way, if the ground is amenable, is to pin the end of the stick down to the ground without adding any great load to it. A common way of doing this is to take a straight shoot with a side branch, keeping 8–12 in. (20–30 cm) above the fork. Point it on the main branch of the fork and bevel the bottom. This can then be hammered into the ground, with the inverted side branch holding the end of the waugun in place. Note that the aim is only to stop the stick from rising up, not to press it down into the ground. You can stop hammering the forked stick as soon as it comes into contact with the waugun. This has applicability to more-complex pot-hanging systems too.

1. *The log spreads the load and prevents the waugun stick from cutting into the ground.*

2. *To prevent damage to the forest floor, we lit our fire on a dried-up side channel of the river we were canoeing. The pot stick was inserted into the base of the bank and supported by a rock.*

3. *Using a forked stick to pin down the end of a waugun stick.*

4. *Students have improvised here by adding a short Y-shaped upright to support the waugun-stick.*

5. *Making use of the wall of an existing fire circle and the base of a pile of rocks constructed as a seat or table. This whole area is underlain by a substrate of solid rock that would never accept wooden sticks, so alternative solutions need to be found.*

1

2

A Spanning Pot Stick

This is a mechanically simpler solution than the aforementioned wauguns, which need holding up off the ground as well as holding down to the ground at the other end. By contrast, this spanning method can consist of a single long, slender pole. It is a pot stick that sits on the ground on one side of the fire and is supported on the opposite side of the fire. There is no upward leverage created. As long as the support is stable, this is the most stable simple waugun. The support can be on a rock or tree stump if one is situated in a convenient place.

Alternatively, and more generally applicable in the woods, one takes an upright supporting stick and drives it into the ground. The closest this upright should be positioned to the fire is one good step away, so that the upright not be consumed by the fire. This waugun-stick setup has the added advantage of some adjustability, although it is not as efficient in this respect as the truly adjustable pot hangers described later in this chapter. By sliding the stick back and forth, you change the angle of the stick and thus the height of the pot hanging from its middle. All you need do to prepare the main, long stick is remove any side branches and cut a notch in the middle section to retain the handle of a pot or kettle. This stick should be 8–9 ft. (2.4–2.75 m) long, at least an inch (2.5 cm) thick, and green. The latter is important, since it will be spanning the fire.

Moving the stick back and forth, or simply making a few notches carved at intervals allowing you to move the pot back and forth relative to the stick, would allow a certain freedom to adjust the pot lower or higher. But you might also have to shift the fire somewhat to ensure it was still under the pot. Also, given the gradual angle of the stick, you may not be able to move the pot vertically as much as you would like. If you want better adjustability, particularly if you are going to be carving several notches, then you are likely better off applying a truly adjustable pot hanger design, such as an adjustable waugun with beaked notches, or a tripod. In either case, the pot can be properly moved vertically without complication.

In terms of removing the pot from the described spanning pot stick, it is best to lift the higher end of the stick, leaving the lower end on the ground to act as a pivot. Then swing the free end of the stick laterally, taking the pot from being over the flames. Then lower the top end of the stick until the pot is on the ground.

1. *Start by cutting a crescent notch in the long stick, no closer to an end than one-third of its length.*

2. *Orient the stick like so, with the stop of the crescent notch on the downhill side of the slope.*

3. *Establish an upright no closer to the fire than a good step away from it.*

4. *Lay the stick on the upright, with the notch over the fire to get an idea of where the stick will need to be positioned to put the pot directly over the fire.*

5. *Lift the supported end of the stick and run the pot handle down it.*

6. *Ensure the pot handle is on the notch.*

7. *Put the top end of the stick back on the upright. You can raise the height of the pot by lifting the top end, then sliding the stick (and pot) back toward the post.*

8. *This is a very stable system with sufficient adjustability for many uses.*

9. *Lifting the top end of the stick to free it from the upright, before swinging it to the side.*

10. *Having swung the stick to the side, lower it to place the pot on the ground. The stick can then be pulled out from between the pot and its handle.*

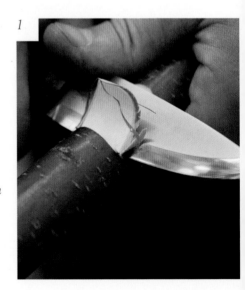

1

Adjustable Pot Hangers

To gain some degree of variability in the heat that you can apply to your camp kettle or cooking pots, you'll need adjustability in the cooking rig or crane you are using. Adjustable pot hangers are an extension of the pot sticks we examined in the previous section, essentially becoming less of a static entity. For example, if we take the spanning pot stick we examined but move the long stick so it is supported in its middle by the upright, then we have something more like a seesaw. Using a clever trick with string, our new seesaw pot hanger can be formalized into an adjustable crane.

The Adjustable Crane

Bernard S. Mason attributes the invention of this type of crane to a gentleman named Stuart Thompson. String is attached to one end of the long stick, and this is pegged down to the ground below, setting the lower extent to which the crane will descend. At the other end of the stick, a notch is cut to retain a pot handle. If the central support needs bolstering, pegs can be driven into the ground around the base, or add just a couple, then tie a length of cord around them and the upright, clamping them together. Clove hitches are very useful in this construction.

1. *The adjustable crane.*

2. *The upright acts as a fulcrum.*

3. *A crescent notch toward one end. Note the orientation of the notch.*

4. *Cord is attached to the opposite end to the notch.*

5. *The cord is then pegged down to the ground.*

6. *The height of the pot is set by adjusting the number of string wraps around the stick.*

7. *With the string at its fullest extent, the crane will set the pot at its lowest.*

8. *The crane with the pot set to low height.*

9. *With the string wrapped once, the crane will be set at the middle height.*

10. *The crane with the pot set to middle height.*

11. *With the string wrapped twice, the crane will set the pot at its highest.*

12. *The crane with the pot set to high.*

The Adjustable Waugun with Beaked Notch

Essentially this pot-hanging system takes the most basic fixed-height waugun-stick, adding an upright for support, fixes securely the grounded end, then adds a component that allows adjustability. This additional component is a tick-shaped (looking like a check mark) pothook that sits on the end of the waugun at one of several possible heights. The setting of height is enabled by carving a series of beaked notches in the pothook. By chamfering the end of the waugun to accept a beaked notch, a pot or a kettle can be hung at any of the heights made possible by the notches.

The proportions of this setup are important. The upright should be positioned at least a step away from the fire, but not much more. If there is a significant length of the waugun proud of the support, there will be excessive flex between the support and the pothook. This makes the hook less stable when attached. If the waugun stick is too short overall, it sits at too steep an angle. It needs to sit at a gradual angle. This has three benefits. First, it is easier to mate the beaked notches onto the chamfered end, the top of which should sit horizontally, or just rising from horizontal. Second, the less like a seesaw the contraption is, the less leverage is applied to the ground end of the stick. This means it is relatively easy to hold down. As long as the upright is solid, this type of hanger can hold remarkably heavy loads. There is no issue with a well-constructed adjustable waugun holding a 2-gallon (10 liter) kettle or a cast-iron Dutch oven full of stew.

1. *The basic structure is a long waugun supported by an upright near the fire and held down at the far end. Then we add a pothook that can sit at various heights.*

2. *Note the proportions, in particular how much length of the main stick there is between the ground and the upright support. If the stick is too short, it sits at too steep an angle.*

3. *A tick-shaped pothook is suspended from the end of the waugun stick.*

4. *Detail of the beaked notch sitting on the end of the waugun stick.*

5. *How a beaked notch mates with a single-stick pot hanger or waugun.*

6. *A well-constructed adjustable waugun with beaked notches can hold remarkably heavy loads, such as this cast-iron Dutch oven.*

7. *This type of pot-hanging arrangement also provides some space and structure for keeping organized with pots and utensils.*

How to Carve a Beaked Notch

The beaked notch is a key component of the adjustable waugun. Moreover, if you are creating a more elaborate cooking setup, then you may want to suspend multiple pots over the fire, each at a different height, which the beaked notch will facilitate.

The beaked notch allows the creation of a pot hanger that is easily raised or lowered, even with the pot attached. If the notch is created and set up correctly, it can hold relatively heavy loads while remaining remarkably stable.

You'll need to create a tick-shaped hanger of a length suited to the application. Look for a straight-growing shoot of a shrub or tree (hazels, willows, and chestnuts are particularly well suited). The shoot you are looking for also needs to have a side branch. Keep the main shoot long and truncate the side shoot near the junction with the main shoot. Also trim any excess material from the main stem below the join. Then you are ready to add the beaked notches.

1. *You'll need a straight shoot with a side branch such as this.*

2. *Truncate the side branch to about an inch (2.5 cm).*

3. *You now have your tick (check mark) shape. This forms the basis of the pot hanger. Now it needs some notches.*

Carving the Beaked Notches

The notches should be carved on the same side of the stem as the tick. This provides balance and stability to the pot hanger. Pay attention to this, since it's a common mistake to carve the notches on the opposite side. A more nuanced detail is that you should try to accurately center your beaks to align them all with the base of the hook from which the pot or kettle hangs.

1. You start the notch by creating an X, centered on an imaginary vertical line running from the base of the hook, up the side of the stick that will have the notches. This is the first cut.

2. The second cut completes the X. These are effectively stop cuts.

3. Here is the X. This allows you to position the notch precisely.

4. Now to start removing some material. Initially this needs to be done carefully, since your stop cut is not very deep. You'll risk slicing too far if you are not deliberate at this stage. Note the position of the hook at the bottom end of the pot hanger and that I'm cutting away from it.

5. Material removed.

6. After a slice or two, deepen the stop cut. Then you can slice out more material with greater confidence.

7. Now slice material from the other side of the X. You should keep the triangle of material at the top of the X intact (N.B.: the top of the hanger is at the bottom left of this photo).

8. Again, deepen the stop cut on this side.

9. Remove more material, cutting into the stop cut but not beyond.

10. After slicing, keep going back to tidying up the edges of the cuts.

11. By alternating this way, you'll be able to slice material out from the area, with an increasingly solid stop cut that also forms the edge of your beaked notch.

12. Now go back to the first side of the X and remove more material.

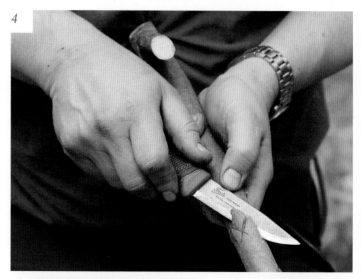

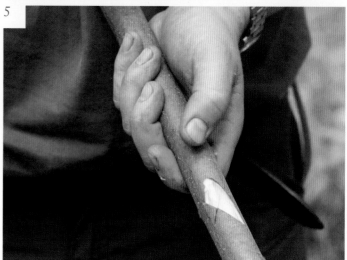

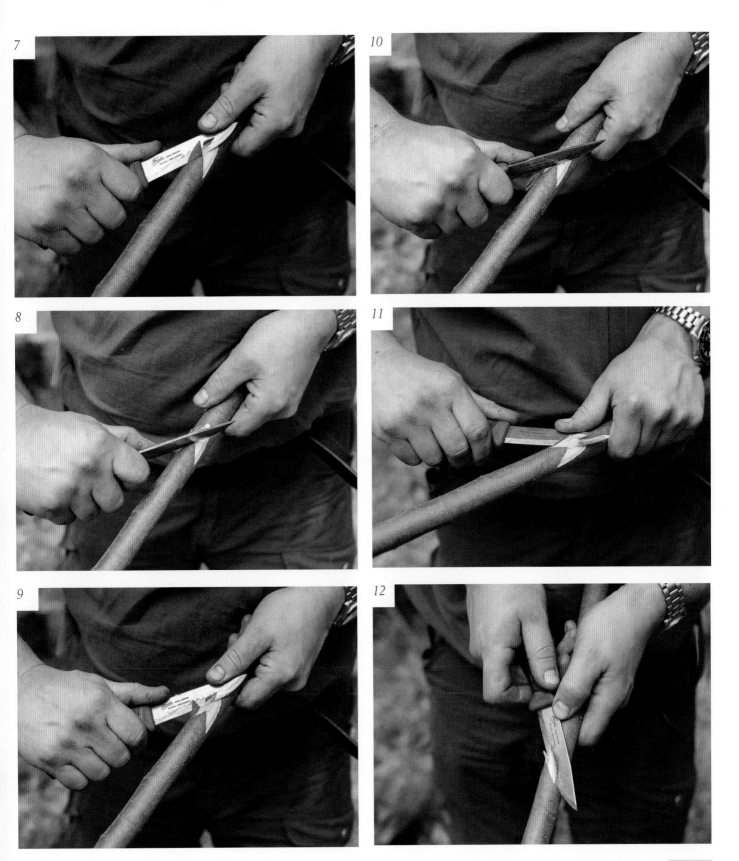

13. Remember to deepen the stop cut as well as keep everything tidy.

14. Once the cuts become established, you can start to undercut them slightly.

15. Keep slicing out material until the notch is deep enough.

16. The beaked notch is taking shape.

17. Make some finishing touches to deepen the notch if necessary. Remember to keep everything symmetrical.

18. Note the ridge under the beak. I haven't directly shaved any material out from under the beak. The undercut here results from the intersection of the two undercuts that meet at the beak.

19. Side view of the beaked notch. You can clearly see the effect of undercutting the stop cuts here.

20. This illustrates the importance of creating the notch on the same side as the hook at the bottom of the hanger. It allows the center of the pot to sit directly under the point where the two sticks fit together.

Adjustable Waugun—Some Useful Variations

There are some useful options in case the base form described previously has some issues, particularly with ground conditions. It may be that pinning down the low end of the stick is tricky for any number of reasons, such as a rock or a tree root impeding things, or you just can't find a suitably forked stick. One alternative is to place a heavy object on the stick. A useful option here is to keep the top branches attached to the sapling you use for making the waugun, and lay them down on the ground. Then place a heavy item on top of the branches to hold everything in place. If the upright is not solid or stable, possibly due to soft ground, you can use two forked sticks to make a variant of the upright support, making the overall structure more like a tripod.

1. *The low end of the waugun shown here has a large log holding it down.*

2. *The birch sapling from which this waugun is made still has its top branches, which are being held down by a log.*

3. *Detail of the low end, with the log on top of the birch sapling's branches, making an effective and stable anchor.*

4. *This waugun has two supports, set at an angle to the vertical, providing a high degree of stability even if they are not inserted far into the ground.*

5. *Detail of intersecting, effectively making the structure a tripod.*

Larger Pot-Hanging Systems

While the simple pot sticks and adjustable hangers provide a range of options, especially for solo campers or small groups, they don't serve all situations. Ground conditions, available materials, group size, or the complexity of the cooking all are significant factors that may leave the more simple waugun sticks wanting.

Tripods

In the pot-hanging hierarchy, tripods have a lot going for them. Tripods are naturally very stable. They are adjustable simply by moving the legs closer in or farther out. Tripods are freestanding, so they work well on rock, snow, sand, pebbly beaches, and any surface where hammering uprights into the ground is not useful or feasible.

A tripod in use on exposed rock typical of the Canadian Shield region.

While I have included tripods in this section on larger pot-hanging systems, don't think they can be used only for big pots or large groups. If you can't put a stick in the ground for a simple waugun, then you have to come up with another solution. A smaller tripod is a solution for even a small pot when on hard ground. It may be the case that there is no soil in the area you wish to camp, but it may also be the case that it is much safer to have a fire out on bare rock than on thin or light soil in among needled trees, for example.

A smaller tripod in use to cook a meal for two when there was nowhere to put a stick in the ground due to very thin or nonexistent top soil.

Tripods have further advantages that make them worth considering under any circumstance. As long as the tripod is tall enough, access to the fire is very good from any angle. Indeed, the tripod does not take up much room around the fire, since it is mainly over the fire. Nor does a tripod take up much floor space under a tarp, whereas a long waugun stick can get in the way in some camps. Wind direction changes, and so does the direction of smoke and hot air from the fire. Being able to access the fire from any side is useful in this respect, to avoid heat, smoke, and sparks when cooking. Like other pot-hanging systems, tripods also provide some structure and space for keeping organized around the fire and the camp kitchen. In particular, the top of a tripod is a good place to hang cups, utensils, and fire gloves.

Next page: Settling in for the night in a wild camp by a river in Ontario, Canada.

Tripods allow good access to the fire from all sides.

The top of a tripod is a good place to store small items you want to keep by the fire.

It's worth considering two separate constituents of the system as a whole: the tripod structure itself and the pothook that hangs from it. While you can make a tripod from three straight, featureless sticks, any tripod is fundamentally structurally sound if the sticks are mechanically connected by more than string. Having at least two of the sticks holding each other in place by means of interlocking forks or side branches makes the system much more solid. Three is even better and might be sufficiently self-supporting not to need any binding at all.

Tripods have the potential to create a cooking space that isn't solely about using the tripod.

Ideally find at least two sticks that can be interlocked structurally by means of forks or side branches.

If you need to make a binding to hold the sticks together in a trio, then the best option is to make a withy by twisting up a suitable species such as willow or hazel, then tying a clove hitch around the three sticks. Sometimes you might be fortunate enough to find a sapling with a side branch for a pothook, along with being long enough to make the binding and pot hanger all in one. Withy up the top, tie your clove hitch, then take the withy over the top of the hitch and down the other side to lock it all off together. More often you will need to fix the sticks, then create the pot-hanging part independently. After tying off the sticks with a clove-hitched withy, you have any number of pothooks you can apply. Compared to other applications, the aspect that makes them different in the context of a tripod is their length. They need to reach from an attachment at the top of the tripod down to just above the fire.

Detail of a tripod bound with a withy. A pothook was then attached by withying the top of two forks and then wrapping them around each other to form a large fixed loop, hanging from the top of the system. It might look a little messy in a photo, but it is very strong. This is made entirely from willow.

This tripod is bound at the top with a withy, then a separate (very long) pothook has been created by withying the top, creating a fixed loop and hanging the loop off the top of one of the tripod legs.

This system has interlocking tripod legs. The fixed loop of the pothook was then inserted over the ends of a couple of legs before opening out the tripod.

Detail of the fixed loop created by twisting up the top section of the pothook stick so it would bend back on itself. It was then tied off against itself with strips of bark.

Get a free video about the technique for
making withies at
wildernessaxeskills.com/resources

The truncated side branch at the bottom of the pothook needs to be sufficiently robust to hold the heaviest pot or full kettle in camp.

You might be thinking that the issue here is the ability to make withies. This is a skill that takes some practice initially and so isn't available to everyone. Even when one does have the skill to make withies, being able to do so is dependent on finding saplings or shoots of suitable tree species such as willow or hazel. This is less likely than finding suitable sticks for the legs of a tripod. So, on canoe trips where I know I will be using tripods at least some of the time, I pack a chain in the kitchen set. This chain can act to bind the tripod legs together, as well as forming the basis of how the pot is hung.

Tripod with chain hanger in use. (Photo by Ray Goodwin)

Binding the tripod legs with a chain. (Photo by Ray Goodwin)

The bottom hook is attached to a ring that can run along the chain, not fixed to the chain. (Photo by Ray Goodwin)

Here, the chain is hooked back onto itself with a hook attached to the free end of the chain. This can be set higher or lower, raising or dropping the pot. (Photo by Ray Goodwin)

Larger arrangements with crossbeams allow multiple-pot cooking over the fire.

Cooking Rigs with Crossbeams

It is possible to modify a large tripod by lashing a crossbeam between two of its legs to create a waugun from which to hang multiple pothooks. A larger option still is to use a tripod as one support point for a crossbeam that spans an elongated fire. The second support can be another tripod, or a bipod. The tripods in these structures don't have pothooks hanging from them directly, but the binding options discussed still apply. Don't bind the crossbeam onto the tripod or in with the legs. You'll want to be able to pass fixed loops on the top of the pothooks over the end of the beam and along its length. Crossbeams can also be added inside group shelters, from which pothooks can be suspended over a central fire.

Once you have a crossbeam, it is possible to hang multiple pots over the fire, either for bigger cooking capacity or for different uses of the fire; for example, for boiling a kettle with flames at one end of the fire but slow cooking a roast or a stew with coals at the other end. In terms of pothooks, there are many methods and variations of such. Some form fixed hangers, while some form adjustable hangers. Here I include detail on some I use most often.

1. *Multiple Dutch ovens hanging from a single crossbeam in an outdoor kitchen*

2. *There are many methods of suspending a pothook from a crossbeam.*

3. *A withy binds the tripod, and the crossbeam is laid on top. You'll want to be able to pass fixed loops onto the beam.*

4. *Note the asymmetrical layout of the tripod—vertical legs on the side of the fire with an angled leg on the outside of the rig.*

5. *The space created by the tripod is a good area to store pots and other kitchen equipment, since no one walks here.*

The beaked notch has a number of potential uses in a larger setup for creating both fixed and adjustable hangers. To create an adjustable pothook, as before, we need multiple notches. The difference here is that the pothook needs to be longer to reach the crossbeam. Another difference is how the beaked notches attach to the larger system as a whole. Here we create a loop of material, attached to the crossbeam, onto which the beaked notch sits. A critical detail is that the upper part of the stick of the pothook should pass behind the loop, up through it, then sit in front of the beam, not just hang precariously from the beak.

There are a number of ways of creating fixed loops at the top of pothooks for use on crossbeams, some of which cross over with techniques you might want to employ with tripods. The methods I use usually involve making a withy, or at least bending a sapling back on itself. Strips of tree bark (taken from other parts of the structure) provide a useful resource for fastening down loose ends. The clove hitch works well as a tape knot in these circumstances. Fixed-loop pothooks can still provide adjustability by linking them together. You can have a short hook hanging from the beam, then hang any one of a number of different second hooks from it to provide different overall positions above the fire.

1. An adjustable pot hanger, utilizing beaked notches, suspended from a crossbeam on a multihanger setup.

2. There are many ways of creating a loop of material. Here I used paracord. It's far enough above the fire not to be at risk of melting. You could also use natural cordage.

3. Here we used a piece of discarded fencing wire to form the hanging loop. Note how the stick passes behind the loop and in front of the beam.

4. A sapling with two forks at the top twisted around itself to form a fixed loop, then fastened off with a bit of bark.

5. Detail of the loop. These are not withies, just intertwined enough that they won't slip.

6. A quick clove hitch to fasten one of the ends against the other fork.

7. Fixed loops created by twisting to increase flexibility, then bending the shoot back on itself. They are tied-off strips of bark from wood elsewhere in the shelter.

8. Note the middle hanger here is two separate fixed-loop hangers daisy-chained together.

9. This material is not flexible enough to be twisted up, but it can be passed across itself, then bound with bark to create a fixed loop.

10. Note the pothook does not hang directly on the bark binding. The downward force tries to pull the sticks apart, exerting a horizontal force on the binding, which is the direction it is strong.

Benches and Seats

Benches and seats are something you might want to consider for a semipermanent camp, especially one you come back to periodically. We have benches in our teaching camps at my bushcraft school. When we are not there, the benches are dismantled and stacked. There are a couple of methods of producing seating that I think are worth knowing.

Split-Log Benches

This type of bench is relatively straightforward to make and requires no equipment other than an axe and a bow saw or bucksaw. This design does require logs to be split lengthways. This is covered toward the end of chapter 4 (see page 120). Once you have a log split down the middle, the rest is really very straightforward.

1. *Use your axe to tidy up the surface of the split log so it's relatively flat, smooth, and not going to introduce splinters into your backside.*

2. *Using your axe, chop two notches into the rounded side of the half log that will accept sawn round logs on which the bench top will sit.*

3. *Here another type of bench can be seen in the background. In this example, two rounds are placed with a vertical orientation and a plank placed across them. It seems a simple design, but creating a flat, parallel-sided plank is difficult with only an axe and bow saw. This plank was cut freehand with a chainsaw.*

4. *As you cut your notches, check that you are achieving a good fit. Once you are satisfied that the bench is stable, then you are done.*

5. *Here you can see split-log benches as part of a seasonal camp that the author uses every year.*

Seats with Legs

Another option, which also makes use of a split log, is one where legs are added to provide a higher seat than a split-log bench seated on two log rounds. These take more-precise work to manufacture, require a specialist tool, and are not as robust or long lived as the simple split-log bench. They have the advantage of not giving you what we term "bench back" as quickly as a low bench, though. You can also make a small version that effectively becomes a stool. Whichever size of legged seat you make, the specialist tool you will need is a Scotch-eyed auger. Fundamentally this is an auger bit with a piece of piping attached to the top that will accept a handle (which you make yourself from a stick in the woods). The tips of the augers I use have a little self-tapping screw thread to help get them started.

1. *A Scotch-eyed auger.*

2. *Detail of the self-tapping screw thread on the tip of the auger.*

3. *Using the Scotch-eyed auger to drill a hole while making a stool.*

To attach legs to your seat or stool, you will need to drill holes into the log, which will accept the legs. The legs should be made of green material or very sturdy seasoned sticks. You have two options of how to attach the legs. The first, and most obvious, is to drill a hole right through the seat, insert a leg with a taper toward the top, then fasten the leg by wedging it from above once the leg is in place. The second option is to create what one might term a blind wedge joint, one where you can't see the top of the leg. This is less obvious and

a little clever. You drill a hole in the underside of the seat, drilling only so far and leaving a solid stop at the top of the hole. Make sure the leg fits quite snugly and only just reaches the limit of the hole. You then make a split in the leg, followed by inserting a wedge into the split, with only a small amount protruding from the top of the leg. When you push, or hammer, the leg into the close-ended hole, the wedge is pushed fully into the leg, which pushes outward into the sides of the hole, thus fastening the leg tight.

4. *Knocking wedges into the top of legs that have been fitted right through the split log. Note the taper toward the top of the log.*

5. *Almost complete, this will be a four-legged bench seat. Once the legs are wedged, you use a saw to cut the top of the legs flush with the surface of the seat.*

6. *After a leg has been tapered and split, here a wedge has been inserted, but it is too long. The knife marks where it needs to be sawn off before being fitted as a blind wedge joint.*

7. *The leg is then hammered into the predrilled hole.*

8. *With the leg fitted and held fast, you can see there is no joint or hole on the top of the seat with the blind wedge joint.*

As a small seat, a stool is more stable on uneven ground with three legs. Longer benches need four legs. Make sure the angles of the three stool legs all splay in different directions.

Large Pegs

For the woodcrafter, a large peg suitable for big tents, group tarps, or parachute shelters is straightforward to make.

While taking a round of wood, pointing one end, beveling the other, and hammering it into the ground is often all that's needed to create a functional peg, sometimes a little more is required. For larger structures, you need a peg that will really hold the ground, will not move laterally, and can work with a relatively upward pull coming from the use of poles causing guylines to approach the ground at steep angles. If you can split out some rounds of wood into quarters or, if the wood is quite large in diameter, eighths, then you can make a clutch of these large pegs in short order. Mathematically the cross section of these pieces is a sector of a circle. They look like a slice of pie. You'll start creating the notch by cutting across the sharp end of the pie wedge.

1. *Start with your piece of split wood by cutting across the grain at the sharp end of the pie wedge to create a stop cut a couple of inches from the top.*

2. *Then cut down to the stop cut in an analogous way to create a crescent notch, just here with the axe.*

3. *Keep deepening the stop cut each time.*

You'll notice that the peg is quite flat on the back. This is the side that faces the structure you are pegging out or pegging down. The breadth of the back of the peg helps prevent it from being pulled through the ground. The notch helps positively retain the guyline cord, whatever the angle it approaches the peg. It's still worthwhile angling the peg away from the guyline a bit though. Otherwise, an almost vertical pull on the peg is effectively placed into the top of the notch, which, in extremis, can split off the part of the peg above this. This is because all that is holding things in place is the glue between the growth rings in the peg. Angling the peg puts these forces more across the grain than along the grain, thus making the guyline more secure.

4. *Once the notch has been completed, start carving a taper on the same side of the peg as the notch.*

5. *Vary the angle of the piece to vary the angle of the cut.*

6. *Now taper in the sides somewhat, aiming for a more defined point at the bottom of the peg.*

7. *Work the angles of the point at the base.*

8. *Lay the peg on its side and use the axe as a heavy knife to bevel the edges of the top.*

9. *Cutting away the ends of the fibers on the outside of the peg means it is less likely to split when struck into the ground.*

Large Tarp Setups

Putting up larger tarps so that they don't flap around in the wind or bow under a load of pooled rain is something of a skill. Fundamentally it comes down to getting the ridgeline and the guylines tight enough. You also need to get the ridgeline high enough so that you are not bent double under the tarp. You also need to set the edges and corners of the tarp at an appropriate angle and height.

A large tarp, complete with adjustable waugun, split-log benches, and a host of other campcraft details.

Setting Up Your Ridgeline

Select a couple of suitably spaced trees between which you can span your tarp. The tensioning system below needs a little extra space beyond what is required just to fit your tarp. You should note that the tensioning system works best with static rope as opposed to dynamic (i.e., stretchy) rope.

Note that for the purpose of demonstrating the system, I have tied the knots low down so that they can easily be seen and photographed. In reality, in setting up a large tarp that I want to walk under, I would be setting this ridgeline up as high as I can reach. Tying knots at arm's length above your head also influences the choice of knots.

Start by securing your rope to one of the trees with a timber hitch. The great thing about the timber hitch is that however much tension is put on the rope, the hitch will come apart very easily as soon as there is no longer any tension.

1. *Start with a timber hitch. Pull the rope tight and test that it holds.*

Tensioning the Ridgeline

When setting up the ridgeline for a small or lightweight tarp for sleeping—under which you need only to sit up at most—tension the line by pulling on it, possibly applying a bit of bodyweight, before tying it off with something like a taut tarp hitch.

With a larger tarp for a covered communal or work area, you would set it higher than head height, and the rope may also be heavier. So, it may be difficult to tension the rope sufficiently just by trying to pull the rope tight, particularly since the tarp may be heavier too. To help, you can set up a simple system that gives you some mechanical advantage in tightening the rope—effectively a pulley system.

You need a system that is easy to untie, even if it has been under a lot of tension, which avoids having to pull all the free rope through the attachment point you are going to use, and which does not damage the rope due to friction. Start by employing a wagoner's hitch, then add a carabiner.

2. *Here you can use a wagoner's hitch to create a loop to pull on.*

3. *To avoid friction on the loop, employ a carabiner.*

4. *Pass the carabiner into the fixed loop. Take the live end of the rope and put this into the carabiner. The other advantage here is that you do not have to pull all of the rope through the carabiner, since it is not a fixed loop.*

5. *Screw the carabiner closed.*

6. *You now have a tensioning system with a 3-to-1 mechanical advantage.*

7. *Here is the full tensioning system.*

There is one potential issue to address. It goes back to the fact that the wagoner's and other knots of this nature, such as the sheepshank, are unstable under lots of tension. Specifically, the loop created by turning the rope like a key, which is passed over the bight, can flip, releasing the bight and causing the system to collapse.

Collapse of the system can be avoided, however, as follows:

8. *Create your horizontal wagoner's hitch as before. Now take a baton and pass it through the bight, above the loop that has been passed over it.*

9. *Cinch up the bight or the loop (or both) so that the baton is held in place by the rope.*

10. *You can now pull as hard as you like on the system, and the sheepshank will not collapse.*

Once you have enough tension in the rope, you will need to tie off the live end to fix everything in place. This can be done by taking a turn around the tree you have used as one end of the span of your ridgeline, then tying off with a couple of half hitches. Remember, though, that most of the time you will be tying this system above head height to provide room under the tarp. To tie off lower down, you need to find another tree farther back than the uprights between which your ridgeline is spanned. Then bring the rope down to the desired height on this third tree.

11. *Bring your rope down as low as you like on the third tree. Finish off with a couple of half hitches.*

8

9

10

11

Setting the Guylines

Once you have your guyline attached, you will want to set the corner of your tarp to the desired height before tying off the guyline. The easy way to do this is by using a pole at the corner of the tarp.

The other advantage of using a pole is that the angle of the guyline to the ground can be sharper than the angle of the tarp. So you can take the guyline down to the ground to peg it where it is most convenient.

With a large rectangular tarp, it can be difficult to tension the guylines sufficiently to make the tarp taut enough not to pool water when it rains. The solution is to drop one corner of the tarp. The edges of the tarp do not have to be horizontal. If one of the corners is lower, then the water runs to that corner and drips off. We don't lose much width under the tarp either. If we drop opposite corners, then we don't end up with a narrow end and a wide end. The main thing to think about is where you would like to direct the water. If the water is going to run off one corner and then back under the tarp, then that might not be the best corner to drop, especially if your fire is nearby where the water might pool. A secondary consideration is where you want the tarp to be a little higher for access and where you don't mind it being a little lower.

1. *Take the guyline around the pole and back over itself to create an Italian hitch. (Photo by Amanda Quaine)*

2. *Take the pole right up to the corner of the tarp to ensure maximum stability. Note the guyline is pulling in the middle of the angle between the two edges of the tarp, thus producing the most even tension across the sheet of the tarp. (Photo by Amanda Quaine)*

3. *Setting one of the corners lower than the other on each side encourages water to run off one corner rather than pooling on the sheet.*

The Adjustable Guyline Hitch

1. Once the peg has been hammered into the ground, take the guyline around the peg and back up toward the pole and tarp. With enough line between your hand and the corner of the tarp to tension the knot you are about to tie, take the live end of the line across the standing part, underneath it, and back into the space you have just created between the live and standing parts. (Photo by Amanda Quaine)

2. Wrap the live end around the standing part a second time, working back toward the peg. (Photo by Amanda Quaine)

3. Take a third wrap, but this time around both pieces of line coming from either side of the peg, still working down the line toward the peg. (Photo by Amanda Quaine)

4. Pull a bight through this last turn (like finishing off a loop in your shoelaces). (Photo by Amanda Quaine)

5. Cinch it tight and you are left with the lovely adjustable guyline hitch as shown. Pulling the bight through has created a quick-release loop, which will serve you well when you need to dismantle camp quickly and efficiently. This knot can now be slid up and down the standing part of the line between the pole and the peg to adjust the tension of the guyline and obtain an optimally tensioned tarp. (Photo by Amanda Quaine)

With a solid understanding of how to tension the ridgeline, set your guylines at the correct height and angle, and adjust the tension of the tarp, you should be able to set up a robust and reliable communal space wherever your travels take you.

Next page: *This is a square tarp with a central suspension point used on a canoe expedition in Manitoba, Canada, but the principles of tensioning the ridgeline and guylines were exactly the same as shown.*

Some Useful Knots

The Sheet Bend

The sheet bend is a very useful bend; quick and simple to tie but one that holds fast. For joining two ropes of equal thickness, it is more secure than a reef knot. In the doubled form it creates a secure join of two lines of unequal thickness. Both the single and double versions of this bend are useful for attaching lines to closed loops of cord or tape loops, such as those attached to the corners of some tarps.

Campcraft Application—Double Sheet Bend with Quick Release

The sheet bend was originally used to attach a line to a sail. It's equally well suited to attaching a line to a tarp, which can also flap around in the breeze or be under tension due to a wind.

Many tarps have tape loops attached to their corners, and a sheet bend is well suited to attaching to a fixed loop. Since the two pieces being joined together are of uneven diameter, it is better to use a double sheet bend here. In addition, I like to be able to remove the guylines from a large tarp quickly when breaking camp, so I add a quick release to each double sheet bend. Here's how I do it:

1. *Pass the guyline up through the tape loop attached to the tarp.*

2. *Pass the line around the back of the loop and under itself (this has created a single sheet bend).*

3. *Continue to take the live end of the cord around the back of the loop for a second time.*

4. *After the line has passed around a second time, rather than passing the live end under, pass a bight under to create a quick release. Once this is done, you tighten it all down on itself by pulling the standing part of the guyline and the tape loop in opposite directions.*

5. *The finished double sheet bend with quick release securely fastens the guyline to the fixed tape loop of the tarp. This will not detach itself even on the windiest days but is easy to undo with a tug of the quick-release tab.*

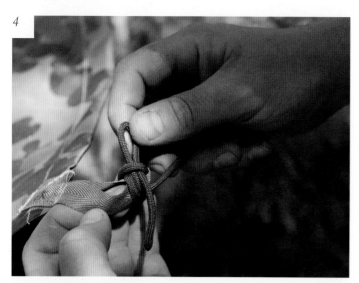

The Clove Hitch

Although this has a very different final appearance to the round turn and two half hitches, the clove hitch also involves two half hitches. As well as attaching a line to a pole or a ring (or carabiner), this visually appealing hitch can also be used as a binding knot, holding together the end of a split stick holding a spatchcock over a campfire, for example.

This is one of the most commonly tied hitches, and definitely one you should have in your repertoire. There are two main ways of tying it, depending on whether the end of what you are tying the clove hitch around is accessible or not. Conversely, you can use one method or the other to tie a clove hitch around a spike, depending on whether the end of the rope is accessible or not.

Method 1—Clove Hitch Tied in a Bight

This method is good for when you have access to the end of what you are anchoring to. You should also note that this method does not require access to the end of the rope.

1. *Start with the rope in each hand.*

2. *Make a crossing turn by passing one part of the rope over the other.*

3. *Take in another length of line similar to the first.*

4. *Make another crossing turn in the same way as the first to create a second loop. The resulting two loops look like mouse ears.*

5. *Pass the second loop behind the first.*

6. *Line up the loops.*

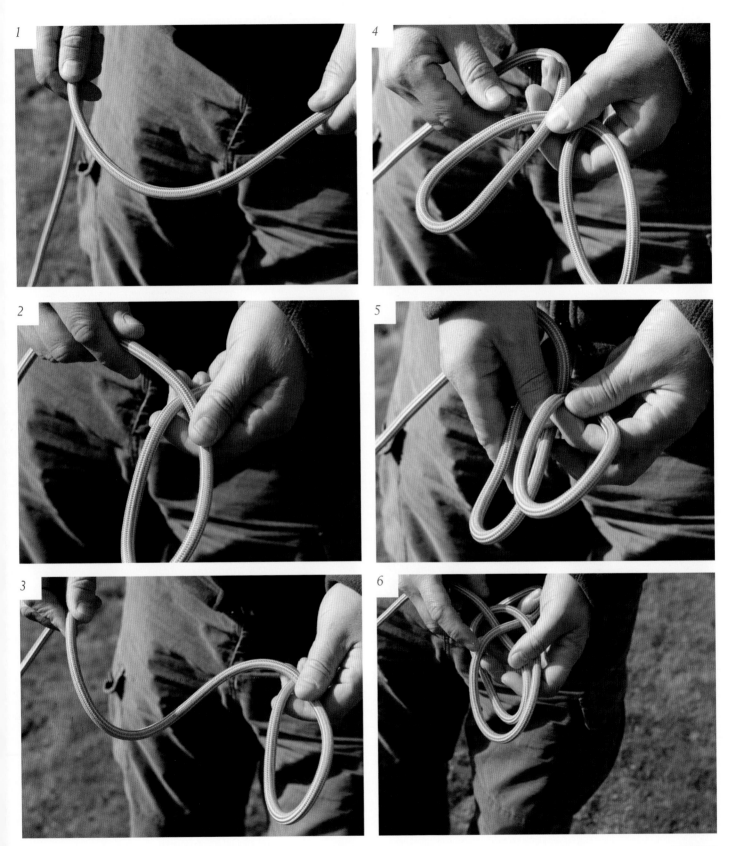

7. *Pass the loops over the end of the anchor.*

8. *While they're still loose, move the loops to where you want the clove hitch.*

9. *Pull each end to tighten the clove hitch in place on the anchor.*

Method 2—Clove Hitch Tied with Working End

This method works well when you have access to the working—or live—end of the rope, or if you do not have access to the end of the anchor (or are attaching to a closed ring).

1. *Pass the live end of the line over the anchor.*

2. *Continue to pass the live end around the back of the anchor.*

3. *Bring the live end to the front again and cross it over the standing part, continuing around the back again.*

4. *Bring the live end to the front once more, maintaining the crossover at the front.*

5. *Pass the live end under the standing part (effectively creating a second half hitch around the anchor).*

6. *Pull the live end up and the standing part down to tighten and complete your clove hitch.*

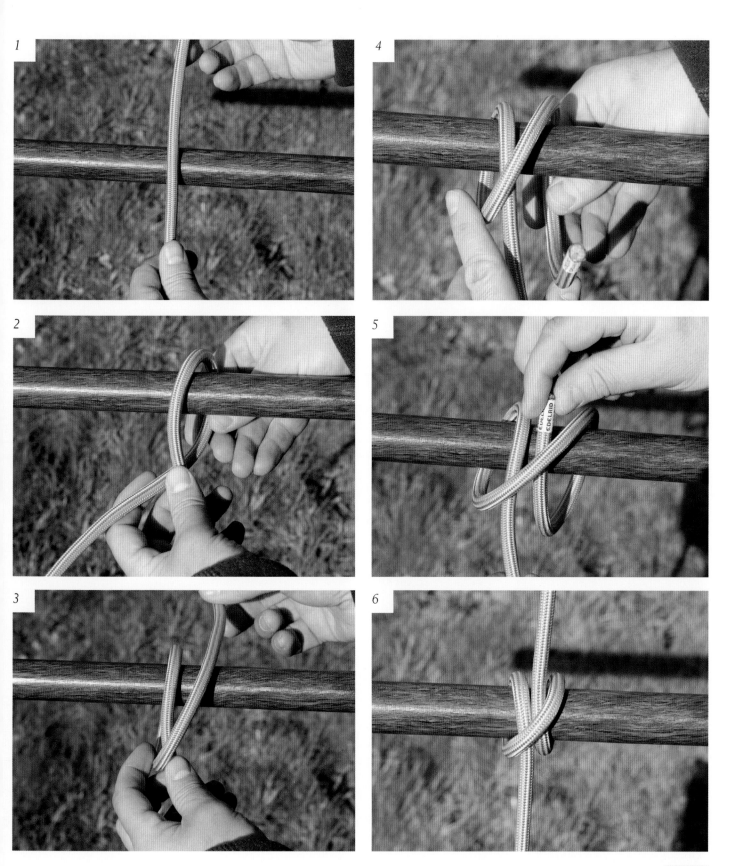

The Italian Hitch

One way of describing the Italian hitch, also referred to as the Munter hitch, is "a clove hitch tied badly." While this is a little unfair, discounting the usefulness of the Italian hitch, it is true this hitch and the clove hitch really differ only in how they are tied by what might seem to the uninitiated like a sleight of hand.

To tie an Italian hitch, make your two mouse ears as per tying a clove hitch in a bight. Then, rather than placing the second loop behind the first (which would result in a clove hitch), fold the two loops in toward each other like you are closing a book. Placing the loops over a spike or onto a carabiner creates an Italian hitch.

Unlike the clove hitch, which will fix the rope in place, the Italian hitch will allow the rope to move. The hitch, however, creates a good deal of friction. Indeed, the Italian hitch is an example of a friction hitch. This can be used to lower loads in a controlled manner or help hoist loads upward. The Italian hitch is neat in that it reverses itself on a carabiner, depending on which end of the rope you pull.

Campcraft Application—Italian Hitch to Hold a Tarp Pole
This is an uncommon application of the Italian hitch, but one I use regularly. Indeed, it is preferable to the clove hitch in this application.

1. *Place a pole at the corner of your tarp, bringing the tarp to the height you want this corner to sit.*

2. *Take the guyline around the pole, then back over itself.*

3. *Continue taking the guyline back to the direction away from the tarp. The result is an Italian hitch around the pole.*

The resultant Italian hitch will hold the pole in place, provided the guyline is tensioned. The pole can also be moved to a new position on the guyline when the tension is released somewhat. When the guyline is untied from the peg or other fixed point, the Italian hitch falls apart with no fiddly untying.

The Constrictor Hitch

If the Italian hitch is a clove hitch tied incorrectly, then the constrictor hitch is a clove hitch with an extra bit added on. These hitches are, of course, all closely related. The interesting thing is how slight changes create a different knot with a different function.

1. *Start by tying a clove hitch, but tie it only loosely.*

2. *Take the free end and cross it over the first loop of the clove hitch.*

3. *Then take the free end under the loop and back into the middle of the hitch.*

4. *You should now have this distinctive shape to the knot, which is a constrictor hitch.*

5. *Pull the free end to tighten the constrictor hitch down on itself.*

The constrictor hitch is an aesthetically pleasing knot. It looks tidy, it bites down on itself, and it's hard to untie. Tie one around your finger and you'll see why it is called a constrictor hitch.